BOSTON

AMERICA'S BEST SPORTS TOWN

SEAN McADAM

FOREWORD BY
PEDRO MARTINEZ

First Edition
First Printing, 2018

Book design by Jake Slavik
Cover design by Jake Slavik
Photographs ©: Julie Jacobson/AP Images, cover (top left), 27; Charles Krupa/AP Images, cover (top middle left), cover (bottom left), 50, 100; AP Images, cover (top middle right), cover (bottom right), back cover (top right), 12–13, 21, 36, 39, 44, 81, 116–117, 140, 156, 162–163; Rick Osentoski/AP Images, cover (top right), 67; J. Walter Green/AP Images, cover (bottom middle left); Bizu Tesfaye/Sipa/AP Images, cover (bottom middle right), 149; ESB Professional/Shutterstock Images, cover (center), 1; Fred Kfoury III/Icon Sportswire/AP Images, back cover (top left), 111; George Grantham Bain Collection/Library of Congress, back cover (top middle left), 78–79; Carlos Osorio/AP Images, back cover (top middle right), 107; Barry Chin/The Boston Globe/Getty Images, 5; Maddie Meyer/Getty Images Sport/Getty Images, 6–7, 57; Damian Strohmeyer/Sports Illustrated/Getty Images, 9, 10, 114; Bruce Bennett Studios/Bruce Bennett/Getty Images, 15, 30, 120, 156, 160–161; A.E. Maloof/AP Images, 18, 3, 166–167; Steve Babineau/National Hockey League/Getty Images, 23; Denis Brodeur/National Hockey League/Getty Images, 26; Brian Babineau/National Hockey League/Getty Images, 28; B. Bennett/Bruce Bennett/Getty Images, 32; Elise Amendola/AP Images, 34–35; Jason Tench/Shutterstock Images, 37; Creative Photo Corner/Shutterstock Images, 41; Cliff Welch/Icon Sportswire/AP Images, 43, 52; Doug Pizac/AP Images, 47; Winslow Townson/AP Images, 49; Harry How/Getty Images Sport/Getty Images, 54–55; Frank O'Brien/The Boston Globe via Getty Images, 59; George Tiedemann/Sports Illustrated/Getty Images, 61; Focus on Sport/Getty Images, 63; Jim Davis/The Boston Globe/Getty Images, 65; Nancy Kerrigan/Getty Images Sport/Getty Images, 71; Timothy A. Clary/AFP/Getty Images, 73; David Durochik/AP Images, 74; Jared Wickerham/Getty Images Sport/Getty Images, 76–77, 104–105; Diamond Images/Getty Images, 83; Rusty Kennedy/AP Images, 87; Jed Jacobsohn/Getty Images Sport/Getty Images, 88; Stan Grossfeld/The Boston Globe/Getty Images, 91; Robert Beck/Sports Illustrated/Getty Images, 92; Ezra Shaw/Getty Images Sport/Getty Images, 94; Corey Sipkin/NY Daily News Archive/Getty Images, 99; Otto Greule Jr./Getty Images Sport/Getty Images, 102–103; Billie Weiss/Getty Images Sport/Getty Images, 110; David Kamerman/The Boston Globe/Getty Images, 113; Jim Wilson/The Boston Globe/Getty Images, 115; Clive Brunskill/Allsport/Getty Images Sport/Getty Images, 119; Bettmann/Getty Images, 123; Bruce Bennett/Getty Images Sport/Getty Images, 125; Eric Schweikardt/Sports Illustrated/Getty Images, 126–127; David Ramos/Getty Images Sport/Getty Images, 129; Al Tielemans/Sports Illustrated/Getty Images, 130–131; Dan Goshtigian/The Boston Globe/Getty Images, 132; Rich Schultz/Major League Soccer/Getty Images, 135; Thomas Shea/Major League Soccer/Getty Images, 137; F.L. Howe/Library of Congress, 138–139; Bill Curtis/The Boston Globe/Getty Images, 142; Andrew Burton/Getty Images Sport/Getty Images, 144–145; Bruce Allen/AFP/Getty Images, 147; John Tlumacki/The Boston Globe/Getty Images, 150; Tim Clayton/Corbis Sport/Getty Images, 151; The Stanley Weston Archive/Archive Photos/Getty Images, 154; Andy Lyons/Getty Images Sport/Getty Images, 156–157, 158–159; Hulton Archive/Archive Photos/Getty Images, 156, 164

Design Elements ©: Shutterstock Images

Press Box Books, an imprint of Press Room Editions, Inc.

Library of Congress Cataloging-in-Publication Data
978-1-63494-027-6

Distributed by North Star Editions, Inc.
2297 Waters Drive
Mendota Heights, MN 55120
www.northstareditions.com

Printed in the United States of America

Author's Dedication

To my father, Robert F. McAdam, who taught me, from an early age and among many other things, about the joys—and more-than-occasional heartbreaks—associated with being a Boston sports fan. He saw the Celtics, Bruins, and even the Patriots win championships in his lifetime, but sadly, missed out on the 2004 World Series win by his beloved Red Sox. I hope it is of some comfort to him that his oldest son was there to chronicle it.

TABLE OF CONTENTS

FOREWORD BY PEDRO MARTINEZ

I remember my first visit to Boston, after I got traded to the Red Sox. It was shocking. The entire Logan Airport was full of people. Their passion and the reception I got were impressive. The curiosity just to see me really stood out and told me Boston was excited about its teams and its players. That gave me some perspective of how it was going to be there.

When I got to Boston, I got a reality check. Right away, expectations were high. I remember being asked on the very first day: "Are you going to replace Roger Clemens?" Right away, I could tell that people expected big things from me. Then I got a couple of "Is this going to be the year that the Red Sox win it all?" Ha—no pressure!

I actually came to Boston well prepared. When I was with the Dodgers, they provided us with someone to teach us English at the complex in the Dominican Republic, and he had graduated from Harvard. He introduced me to the history of Boston. He would put on Red Sox games on the satellite and would teach me about the history of Boston and the culture there. That's probably why I adjusted well.

When I came to Boston, I already knew about the (championship) drought. I knew about most of the players—Jim Rice, Oil Can Boyd, Ellis Burks, Wade Boggs, Dwight Evans. And every pitcher in Boston wanted to be like Roger Clemens. That was probably the only team in baseball where I already knew about its history and tradition. That's what's great about Boston: Everybody knows everything about their team.

Even though I thought I had a pretty good understanding about what Boston was going to be like, the first time I pitched at Fenway was something I couldn't have prepared for. That day showed me how engaged the fans were, how close they were, and how demanding they were going to be. Like everything in life, I decided to look at it as a challenge.

From the beginning, there was a love affair between myself and the Boston fan base. Those fans wanted to see dedication and commitment, and I think they saw that in me. They knew I really cared.

The atmosphere in Boston reminded me of a game between Licey and Aguilas back in the Dominican. People were banging on the wall and chanting, "Let's go, Pedro!"

That never went away. Right away, I knew Boston was probably the only city that would resemble what it was like in winter ball.

And it wasn't just the Red Sox. When I played, I got the opportunity to go see the Bruins, go see the Celtics. I was introduced to Paul Pierce, met Bobby Orr. I got to throw batting practice to Tom Brady once! I've had the opportunity to get close to a lot of Boston sports legends. When you're a pro athlete in Boston, there's a special bond, and I always enjoyed getting together with players from the other teams in town.

These days, I miss the heat, the intensity, the passion that Boston sports fans bring. They're so passionate. And in the last 10 to 15 years, with all the championships won by all the teams, I'm glad the fans have had so much to celebrate. They deserve it.

There's no other city like it when it comes to sports. The fans make it a real community, there are legends everywhere, and the tradition and history are like no other city.

▲ Pedro Martinez's seven shutout innings in Game 3 helped the 2004 Red Sox end the 86-year "curse" with their World Series win over the St. Louis Cardinals.

I'm appreciative of the love the city of Boston has shown me and all people in sports. I don't have enough words to thank Boston—not only for embracing me, but for embracing everyone on the sports scene. They never stop being loyal, and I will never forget them.

Pedro Martinez pitched for the Red Sox from 1998 through 2004, winning two American League Cy Young Awards and the 2004 World Series.

BOSTON
SPORTS TOWN

Why Boston?

That is, why choose Boston as America's greatest sports city?

Surely, other cities can try to make that claim. Other cities have four—or more—pro sports franchises; a vibrant college sports scene; and special, localized events that make them unique. Others have won championships, boasted of superstars, developed histories of their own.

So what makes Boston so special? I'd argue three main factors:

Success.

Tradition.

And passion.

Boston has all three. To spare.

◀ David Ortiz salutes the Fenway Park crowd after his final game with the Red Sox, which came during the 2016 playoffs.

You want to talk about success? No team in NBA history has won more championships than the Celtics. No NFL team has dominated in the 21st century like the Patriots. The Bruins have won three Stanley Cups since 1970, reached the Final six other times, and set a league record for most consecutive trips to the playoffs. And after 86 years of futility, frustration, and agonizingly close calls, the Red Sox won it all in 2004. Then they won twice more in the next nine years.

Tradition? In Boston, fandom is a tradition, handed down from generation to generation. Your grandfather went to Fenway Park and watched Ted Williams. Your father saw Carl Yastrzemski there. And now you go to the same ballpark, built in 1912, to watch the next class of homegrown stars.

But it's not just the Red Sox. Two of Boston's four major franchises—the Celtics and the Red Sox—were charter members, original pieces of their respective leagues. The Patriots were charter members in their own way, an original team in the American Football League. And Boston's fourth team, the Bruins, became the NHL's first US entrant. Heck, even the New England Revolution were among the first class in Major League Soccer.

And you can't talk tradition without talking college sports. Although Boston is first and foremost a pro sports town, the intercollegiate scene boasts deep roots of its own. Elements of modern college football—including mascots, fight songs, and other staples of the game—can be traced to Harvard's nascent program, well over a century ago. Even today, attending a Harvard football game on a crisp, picturesque New England fall day might not be the same as, say, Michigan–Ohio State at the Big House, but it's special nonetheless.

THICK AND THIN In Foxborough, snowfall does little to dampen the spirits of Patriots faithful.

It's not just football, though. In the winter, you can take your pick of national college hockey powers at either end of Commonwealth Avenue or choose from a handful of entertaining college basketball games among the area's four Division I programs. No matter the sport, men's and women's teams from Boston College, Boston University, Harvard, and Northeastern—not to mention the area's smaller schools—each have their own traditions and die-hard fans.

Then there are the other traditions, those that are uniquely Boston. The city has two historic sporting events all its own: the Marathon—no "Boston" needed for the locals— each spring and the Head of the Charles Regatta in the fall. Some local high school football rivalries date back more than a century. And there are homegrown stars who went on to greatness elsewhere—Patrick Ewing and Jeremy Roenick to name two—and remain

BOSTON STRONG Boston sports were never more unified than in the aftermath of the Boston Marathon bombing in 2013.

revered in New England. In short, there's something for everyone: summer and winter, pro and amateur, men and women.

Then there's the passion. Blessed with excellence from their local teams, Boston fans are ready to put their money where their hearts are. Even before they won their first World Series in 86 years, the Red Sox in 2003 began a North American pro sports franchise record by selling out 820 straight games—or every home game for nearly a decade. The Patriots have a waiting list for season tickets that likely won't be filled for decades. And both the Bruins and the Celtics traditionally play to full houses. Fan interest is manifested in other ways, too. The city is home to two all-sports radio stations, and their combined listening audiences account for almost a third of the market share.

The qualities that make Boston a unique sports town were all on display in 2013. When tragedy struck the city during the bombings at that year's Boston Marathon, the city rallied around the Red Sox, who by tradition had finished playing their annual Patriots' Day game less than a mile from the finish line not an hour before the explosions. That season's plucky edition of the Sox introduced "Boston Strong" as their unofficial motto, a tribute to the area's resilience. The team went on to an improbable World Series victory, and in so doing served as an emotional vessel for a city reeling from the attack. Then, the following spring, Meb Keflezighi became the Boston Marathon's first American winner in nearly three decades.

In so many ways, being a sports fan in Boston is as good as it gets. While other cities are in the midst of long waits for their next championship, there are no lengthy droughts for the Boston faithful to endure. Boston fans, by contrast, have enjoyed an embarrassment of riches since the turn of the century. Younger fans believe duck boat parades—the practice of championship teams winding through the city on wheeled boats that can suddenly turn amphibious—to be their birthright.

So go ahead and call us spoiled. We'll happily accept the criticism. We—or our forbearers—have been privileged to watch some of the greats in every game, some so widely known that they're identified by a simple name or nickname: Ted. Yaz. Russ. Numbah Foah. Tommy. Each represents not only the best in Boston, but in some cases the best ever in their respective sports. Try finding another city that can say that about each sport.

These immortals usually performed in front of packed ballparks, stadiums, or arenas. Fan support is taken for granted. The passionate fan base is there, as the old joke goes, win or tie. So forgive us our deep, parochial pride. We think we've earned it.

CHAPTER 1

THE BRUINS

Of the four major pro franchises in Boston, a case could be made that the Bruins, the local NHL entry, best mirror the city's makeup and personality.

Although Boston is widely recognized as the home to elite universities and patrician families who can trace their roots to the *Mayflower*, the city also has a proud working-class history that populates neighborhoods such as Charlestown, South Boston, and the North End. Though each has been beset by modern gentrification, these communities remain close-knit, somewhat tribal, and unfailingly proud of their heritage (largely Irish or Italian).

The region's cold winters made Boston a natural fit to be the first US entrant into the fledgling NHL, formed in 1917. From the Bruins' beginning in 1924, Boston embraced the team, crowding the original Boston Garden in support.

◀ Bruins defenseman Eddie Shore was one of the NHL's first star players.

The Garden, in turn, became the perfect home to the Bruins. Located above a train station and accessible to all thanks to nearby subway lines, the Garden was a cozy, idiosyncratic, democratic arena with questionable sight lines and little in the way of amenities.

The Bruins' first superstar, Eddie Shore, embodied the toughness that would come to be associated with the sport and the franchise itself. Let the Montreal Canadiens boast of flashy goal scorers skating effortlessly down the wing; the Bruins would be represented by a tough-as-nails defenseman who played with a barely disguised fury.

Not that Boston lacked the ability to score goals. Playmaking forward Milt Schmidt centered a line with Woody Dumart and Bobby Bauer that came to be known as the "Kraut Line," an appellation that would be unthinkable in a more politically correct time. Their final game before shipping off to war in 1942 saw the trio combine for three goals and 11 points and ended, incongruously, with the rival Canadiens, having been vanquished in an 8–1 thrashing, carrying the trio around the Garden ice on their shoulders.

This sort of patriotic expression only further cemented the bond between team and fan base. Schmidt and Co. may have been Canadian by birth, but they were all fighting on the side of the Allies.

This was a sport, and a team, that established a connection with the dockworkers, the construction workers, the cops, and the firemen—the blue-collar, hardscrabble class that sought an escape from their workaday existence and found it in the no-nonsense approach of the Bruins.

KRAUT LINE *From left,* Bobby Bauer, Woody Dumart, and Milt Schmidt made up the Bruins' legendary "Kraut Line" during the late 1930s and early 1940s.

The fans expected an honest effort from the team and were seldom disappointed. And when the situation on the ice called for it, the Bruins historically stuck up for one another. Unlike any of the other major sports, hockey's code allowed—encouraged, even—a physical, all-for-one approach, and the Bruins were only too eager to embrace it.

For large chunks of their history, that rough-and-tumble style was all the Bruins offered. The franchise's history was dotted with brief periods of dominance followed by long stretches of competitive irrelevance. Frustration existed, but support seldom waned; the Garden often remained sold out in the Bruins' years in the wilderness, even during a 20-year span from 1947–48 to 1966–67 that saw them enjoy only four winning seasons.

THE FIVE GREATEST GAMES IN
BRUINS HISTORY

5. Farewell to the "Kraut Line" (February 10, 1942)

This 8–1 thrashing of Montreal didn't result in a Stanley Cup, but it proved more memorable in one sense. It was the final game for a while for the famed "Kraut Line" of Milt Schmidt, Woody Dumart, and Bobby Bauer before they went off to fight for the Royal Canadian Air Force in World War II, and the trio went out in style, scoring three goals and 11 points. In an emotional sendoff at a sold-out Boston Garden, the three Bruins were carried off the ice by, of all people, their opponents, who were grateful for their patriotism and service.

4. A Montreal Meltdown—Game 7, NHL Semifinals (May 10, 1979)

The Bruins lost Game 7 of the semifinals to the hated Canadiens and did so in the most painful fashion imaginable. Leading by a goal with four minutes remaining, the Bruins gave up a game-tying goal, then lost in overtime in their own House of Horrors, the Montreal Forum. It was a heartbreaking loss for Bruins fans, but the game was a classic between two rivals, with nearly a dozen future Hall of Famers taking part.

3. The Drought Is Over—Game 7, Stanley Cup Final (June 15, 2011)

Like the Cup winner that preceded it, the Bruins clinched this title with a shutout, blanking the Canucks 4–0 to end the franchise's 39-year championship drought. The win culminated a strange series, with three of the games closely contested and settled by a single goal and four others won by margins of three, four, four, and seven goals.

2. Second in Three Years—Game 6, Stanley Cup Final (May 11, 1972)

For the second time, Bobby Orr scored the Cup-clinching goal, this time in the first period of a 3-0 shutout of the Rangers in Game 6 at Madison Square Garden. This one wasn't as dramatic as the 1970 clincher, but little did anyone know this would be the last B's Cup winner for almost four decades.

1. The Dive—Game 4, Stanley Cup Final (May 10, 1970)

On Mother's Day, the Bruins won their first Stanley Cup in 29 years as Derek Sanderson fed a pass from behind the net to Orr, who flicked it past Blues goalie Glenn Hall just 40 seconds into overtime. Just as Orr was lifting his stick in celebration, he was tripped by a Blues defenseman, sending him through the air and resulting in one of the most iconic photos in sports history.

But on occasion, when the Bruins experienced winning while still maintaining their trademark style of play, the bond they created with the city was unmatched. The fans' affection for the Bruins of the late 1960s and early 1970s might never be topped—not by the dynastic Celtics of the 1960s and 1970s, not by the curse-busting Red Sox of the early 21st century, and not by the Patriots' reign of dominance that began with Belichick and Brady.

There was little that a loyal Bruins fan wouldn't endure. But that doesn't mean ownership couldn't test the fan base's patience. An ugly salary dispute with the franchise's greatest player ever, Bobby Orr, led to the unfathomable in the mid-1970s: the hockey icon wearing the sweater of another NHL team. Later, as salaries rose, the Bruins stubbornly held the line on payroll, refusing to acknowledge the game's changing economic landscape.

The product suffered, and for a while so did attendance. It didn't help that penurious owner Jeremy Jacobs came to be known as one of the league's most hawkish voices, holding the line on soaring salaries and contributing to three work stoppages.

Eventually, the league got its economic house in order. In recognition of a new labor landscape and the demands from the fan base to assemble a competitive product, the Bruins spent to the top of the salary cap. Finally, in 2010–11, the Bruins' long championship drought ended with a dramatic Game 7 victory at Vancouver. A crowd estimated at more than a million lined the streets of Boston for the city's first Stanley Cup parade since the Nixon administration and served as a vivid reminder of the team's heritage and long-running support.

The love affair, threatened at times, was again in full bloom.

The Big Bad Bruins
Rule the Town

For those not old enough to have lived through the era of the Big, Bad Bruins of the late 1960s and early 1970s, it might be difficult, if not impossible, to grasp the immense popularity of that team.

Led by the incomparable Bobby Orr and with a supporting cast that included three Hall of Famers (Phil Esposito, Gerry Cheevers, and Johnny Bucyk) and a host of perennial All-Stars (Ken Hodge, Johnny McKenzie, and Dallas Smith), the Bruins captured two Stanley Cups and made another trip to the Final in the span of five seasons.

Beyond the team success was an entertaining style of play and a slew of larger-than-life personalities. The Bruins scored a record 399 goals in 1970–71, with just 207 against. Montreal, the next best team, scored just 291 goals. That year's Bruins also set a record for most players with 20 goals or more in a season, with 10 players reaching that milestone.

And when those Bruins weren't burying pucks at a record pace, they were landing punches and dishing out punishing checks. Never before had a hockey team played with such a lethal combination of skill and toughness, of pure ability and brawn.

The combination of highlight-reel goals and grit were enough to capture the city's affection, in part because of the lack of real competition for the hearts and minds—to say nothing of the wallets—of the region's fans.

Before their half-dozen seasons' reign as the NHL's most successful and entertaining team had ended, they were responsible for the launch of an independent TV station, TV 38, which first gained traction as the flagship station of the B's, and the construction of a number of municipally supported ice rinks throughout the greater Boston area, which begat a generation of youth hockey players, planting the seed for generations to come.

There also existed an undeniable bond between the team and its fan base, which was predominantly blue collar. It was those fans with whom the Bruins connected. They identified with the team's toughness, its work ethic, and, yes, its willingness to avenge a wrong done to a teammate. The 1973 film *The Friends of Eddie Coyle* perfectly encapsulated this relationship with its famous scene in which the titular character, played by Robert Mitchum, rhapsodizes about the brilliance of Orr from his seat with the rest of the Gallery Gods—the nickname bestowed on the fiercely loyal fans who occupied the Garden's upper reaches.

How popular were those Bruins? With Bruins tickets impossible to come by, the team's American Hockey League minor league affiliate, the Boston Braves, routinely sold out the Boston Garden. If fans couldn't finagle a way to see Orr and Co., then surely the baby Bruins of the future represented the next best thing. Although rival teams had players who specialized in finesse and others who displayed a thirst for fisticuffs, the Bruins had no such division of labor. Some of their most skilled players, including Orr, harnessed mean streaks and the ability to drop the gloves when needed.

Orr, of course, was the team's centerpiece. He was a transformative player who redefined his position and changed the game in ways too numerous to cite. Until Orr, defensemen were regarded as children at a grown-up party—not to be seen or heard (past the blue line, anyway). Orr served as a change agent, turning defense into offense with a quick pivot and a quicker burst of speed up ice.

Of course, spectacular as he was, Orr wasn't alone.

For a period of eight years, there was no more reliable goal scorer in the NHL than Esposito. Overshadowed on his own team by Orr, Esposito nevertheless established himself as one of the game's most unstoppable offensive forces. Beginning in 1967–68 and ending in 1974–75, Esposito each season led the league in either goals, assists, or points—or, in the case of the 1972–73 season, all three.

Esposito had the size, strength, and courage to plant himself in the slot in front of the opponents' goal, where he suffered relentless physical abuse but also established himself as the game's premier scorer, gathering pucks and potting them into the net. A popular bumper sticker in New England said it best: "Jesus saves . . . and Esposito scores on the rebound!"

As the sports world transformed in the late 1960s to mirror the world around it, the Bruins were emblematic of that culture shock. Suddenly, pro athletes were no longer cardboard cutouts ripped from some Chip Hilton novel—modest to a fault, exceedingly polite, and clean-cut in appearance.

Now, athletes had style and personality. Muhammad Ali had kicked down the door with his unabashed self-promotion and spoke not in clichéd sound bites, but in playful

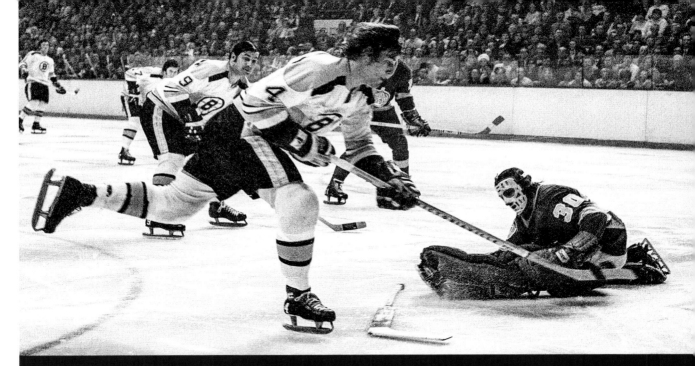

BIG, BAD, AND GOOD Bobby Orr shoots as Hall of Fame teammate Johnny Bucyk (9) looks on during a 1972 game against the Kings.

rhymes. Joe Namath had pioneered the notion of the athlete-playboy, and Derek Sanderson, the B's third-line center, followed Namath's lead (the two would become investors in a series of athlete-owned nightclubs). But beyond their success was the strong sense of bonhomie that radiated from the team. The Bruins were modern-day swashbucklers, determined to have one another's backs on the ice, and equally committed to enjoying life off ice.

"If you fight one Bruin," coach Harry Sinden said of his charges, "you have to fight 18 of them."

Orr, who had arrived with a buzz cut and an almost pathological shyness, evolved into a team leader and unofficial social director. He made postgame visits to a local tavern mandatory, and the B's reveled in their newfound status as the city's most lovable folk heroes. In one notorious incident, following a stunning first-round playoff exit, the Bruins executed a late-night jailbreak of sorts at a local hospital. They wheeled Esposito, still in traction and recovering from recent knee surgery—*hospital bed and all*—across the street to a bar, where they conducted a very liquid end-of-season wake.

Of course, the team wouldn't have been so captivating had it not been for its on-ice dominance. It helped that the NHL's rapid expansion in 1967 had doubled the number of teams from six to 12. Suddenly, the league was full of past-their-prime journeymen and prospects not yet ready for the limelight.

For all of the talent the Big, Bad Bruins possessed, it could be argued that they actually underachieved. Injuries, especially to Orr, who seldom played anywhere near fully healthy after his first few seasons, and defections to the rival World Hockey Association—Sanderson, McKenzie, Ted Green, and Cheevers were all lured away by the promise of far bigger paychecks—limited the B's.

They won two Cups and nearly claimed a third before losing to Philadelphia in 1974, but they fell short of the dynastic runs experienced by the Canadiens in the 1970s and the New York Islanders and Edmonton Oilers in the 1980s.

Then again, a case could be made that those Bruins can't be measured by Stanley Cups alone. Decades later, the Bruins of the late 1960s and early '70s still hold a significant place in Boston sports history—for their impact, their swagger, their unmatched camaraderie, and occasionally, their on-ice brilliance.

Behind the Blue Line

In sports, certain franchises or programs tend to specialize in one position. The Bruins, for whatever reason, have had one great defenseman after another.

The tradition began with Eddie Shore, who was not only the first great Bruins blue-liner but arguably the fledgling league's first true gate attraction and first superstar. Shore came to the Bruins for the start of the 1926–27 season and was part of two Stanley Cup–winning squads a decade apart. He also won the Hart Trophy—awarded annually to the league's most valuable player—an unprecedented four times, the most ever by a defenseman.

Shore was a defenseman in the strictest sense. While Bobby Orr would one day redefine how the position was played and viewed, Shore was far more traditional, focused chiefly on protecting his team's net and unafraid to dish out punishing hits. He frequently was among the league leaders in penalty minutes, and his scoring contributions, typical for the era, were relatively meager.

Above all, Shore was the forerunner of the Bruins' fearless, physical play. Nearly 90 years after the fact, Shore still owns the NHL record for most fighting majors (five) in a single game. Over his career he suffered four broken noses and five broken jaws. He was undeterred by injury and came by his nickname—"Old Blood and Guts"—naturally. He also became a target for opposing players who weren't above placing a bounty on him.

"Everybody was after him," said Milt Schmidt, a onetime teammate and Hall of Famer in his own right. "They figured if they could stop him, they could stop the Bruins."

The approach often backfired. When Shore leveled Toronto's Irvine "Ace" Bailey with a devastating retaliatory hit from behind—Shore thought he was targeting King Clancy, who had decked him a minute earlier—the Leafs' forward nearly died on the ice.

Shore was something of a trailblazer in other ways. He was a tough negotiator when it came time to talk contract, earning him the wrath of GM Art Ross. (Shore's willingness to advocate for his own salary would later prove ironic when, as the unyielding owner of the AHL Springfield Indians, he treated his players like chattel. Such an approach helped lead to the formation of the first players union and, subsequently, Shore's decision to sell his ownership interest in the franchise.)

Then came Orr, and after Orr came Ray Bourque. From the moment he arrived in Boston in the fall of 1979, Bourque seemed destined to live in the largest of shadows.

First, there was the unenviable position of joining the Bruins as a highly touted defenseman only three seasons after Orr—only the greatest to play the position—left the franchise. No one could escape that sort of comparison. Even upon his arrival, Bourque was playing alongside another stud defenseman in veteran Brad Park. Then, there was this: Bourque, as promising a prospect as he was, wasn't the most celebrated newcomer to Boston that fall. That distinction belonged to a gangly basketball player from French Lick, Indiana, named Larry Bird, who made

> "I'll take Orr if I'm down by a goal, but I'd take Bourque if I'm defending a one-goal lead."
>
> - Harry *SINDEN*
> LONGTIME BRUINS COACH AND GM

FIVE TRADES
THE BRUINS DEFINITELY WON

Great teams are built in a variety of ways. But it's worth noting how many transformational players the Bruins have brought in via trade over the years.

5. Terry Sawchuk to Detroit for Johnny Bucyk (July 10, 1957)

Sawchuk was one of the greatest goalies ever, but his best seasons were behind him at the time of this deal, while Bucyk went on to become a 20-goal scorer in 16 of his 21 seasons in Boston. When he retired, he was the fourth-highest-scoring player in league history.

4. Barry Pederson to Vancouver for Cam Neely and a first-round draft pick (June 6, 1986)

Pederson was a nice player, but in return, the Bruins got a haul. The first-round draft pick turned out to be Glen Wesley, a first-pair defenseman who logged seven seasons in Boston. The Bruins also got a Hall of Famer in Neely, who not only came to embody what it means to be a Bruin but also redefined the power forward position in the NHL.

3. Ron Grahame to Los Angeles for a first-round draft pick (October 9, 1978)

Grahame was an ordinary goalie and went on to play just 66 games in net for the Kings. Meanwhile, that first-round pick turned into Ray Bourque, who won five Norris Trophies and is regarded as the second-best defenseman ever to wear the Bruins uniform.

2. Phil Esposito and Carol Vadnais to the Rangers for Jean Ratelle, Brad Park, and Joe Zanussi (November 7, 1975)

The Bruins traded a declining Esposito for Ratelle, who was a more complete player at the time. That Boston essentially got Park for Vadnais, however, puts this deal over the top. The Bruins knew Bobby Orr was near the end of his career because of a series of knee injuries, and Park played eight more seasons, finishing runner-up in Norris Trophy voting two times.

1. Jack Norris, Gilles Marotte, and Pit Martin to Chicago for Phil Esposito, Fred Stanfield, and Ken Hodge (May 15, 1967)

This isn't just the greatest trade in Bruins history; it may well be one of the top five hockey trades of all time. The Bruins got a Hall of Fame center in Esposito, a second-line center in Stanfield, and a winger in Hodge who would score 289 goals in nine seasons in Boston.

▲ Ray Bourque won five Norris Trophies in 21 seasons with the Bruins.

his pro debut with the Celtics that October. Add the fact that English wasn't Bourque's native language, and you get a sense of what he was walking into that autumn.

Somehow, against that backdrop, he made an immediate impact. Bourque enjoyed a fabulous rookie season, setting a record for most points by a rookie defenseman, capturing the Calder Trophy (awarded to the league's top first-year player), and earning first-team All-Star status.

That was only the beginning of a fabulous 21 seasons in Boston, a stretch that would see Bourque become the Bruins' all-time leader in games played and points scored. But he was hardly an offense-only defenseman. With a rugged build (5'11", 219 pounds), Bourque had a physical presence to his game. And blessed with terrific instincts on the ice, he was adept at anticipating developing plays from the opposition.

Although no one will ever match Orr's otherworldly offensive game, it's hardly heresy to suggest that Bourque may have been superior in his own zone. Harry Sinden, who coached Orr and drafted Bourque, was once asked which of the two he would want on the ice in the final minute of a must-win game.

"I'll take Orr if I'm down by a goal," said Sinden, "but I'd take Bourque if I'm defending a one-goal lead."

The Bourque era ended in March 2000 when, at his request, the Bruins traded him to Colorado so the aging star could have one last shot at a Stanley Cup. The move worked out for Bourque, who ended his career by lifting the Cup in 2001. The B's, meanwhile, went several seasons without a standard-bearer on the blue line.

That finally changed in 2006 when the Bruins signed giant free agent Zdeno Chara. At 6'9", 250 pounds, Chara was

▲ Zdeno Chara lifts the Stanley Cup in 2011.

the biggest player to ever lace up skates in the NHL. His contributions to the franchise have also been towering. He was the Norris Trophy winner in 2008–09 as the league's top defenseman, a top-three finalist for the award in four other seasons, and the captain of the Stanley Cup–winning team in 2010–11.

In the modern NHL, there's a need for a "shutdown defenseman"—a player who can be matched up with the opponent's most fearsome forward and be counted on to limit his impact. With Chara's size, ridiculously long reach, and brute strength, he has filled just such a role with the Bruins since his arrival in town. And unlike Park or Bourque, Chara can count himself among the Bruins to have won a Cup in Boston.

The Rivalry: Montreal

For the longest time, it would be a stretch to call what existed between the Bruins and their arch-nemesis, the Montreal Canadiens, a "rivalry." After all, a rivalry suggests some manner of intense, impassioned, equitable relationship. But between the end of World War II and the late 1980s, little was equitable about the Bruins and Canadiens.

There was passion and intensity, to be sure, as would be expected between two of the NHL's Original Six franchises. But equitable? Not by a long shot. Would the "hammer and nail" be considered a rivalry? Because that comes close to conveying how one-sided the Bruins-Canadiens relationship was for more than four decades.

While Montreal was en route to establishing itself as the greatest franchise the NHL had known, with dynastic runs in the 1950s (five straight Cups), 1960s (four in five years), and 1970s (six in nine years), the Bruins won just two Stanley Cups in the span of 67 seasons. Worse for Boston was the head-to-head competition between the teams—if it could, in fact, be considered competition.

Consider: between 1947 and 1987, the Bruins and Canadiens met 18 times in the playoffs, with the same outcome every year: a Montreal victory. It didn't matter if the series took place in the quarterfinals, semifinals, or Cup finals. The result was always the same.

Montreal ending the Bruins' season became a sadly familiar tradition. Like flowers blooming on the Common, or boats sailing the Charles, it became something of a rite of spring. For although there certainly were years in which the Bruins

outperformed the Canadiens and finished well ahead of them in the standings, the B's went 41 long years without beating the Habs in the postseason.

In 1971, with the Bruins clearly the superior team, the Habs took a gamble on a young goaltender fresh out of Cornell University. Ken Dryden, with all of six regular-season games of NHL experience to his credit, turned the B's aside in seven games, and Montreal went on to win yet another Cup, despite having finished 24 points behind Boston.

The absolute low point, from the Bruins' standpoint anyway, was a 1979 semifinal series in which the Bruins carried a one-goal lead into the final minutes of Game 7 in the Forum. But the Bruins were penalized for having too many men on the ice, which resulted in a game-tying goal. In overtime, Yvon Lambert potted the game-winner, and the Bruins' misery was extended for yet another year.

But a closer look at the tying goal reveals the real reason for the Bruins' struggles with the Habs that season. The Canadiens had six players on the ice—Jacques Lemaire, Guy Lafleur, Steve Shutt, Larry Robinson, Serge Savard, and Dryden—and every last one of them was eventually elected to the Hockey Hall of Fame.

This wasn't about officiating or jinxes or karma. This was about talent.

BOSTON BRUINS
MOUNT RUSHMORE

Raymond Bourque (1979–2000)

Bourque had to play in the considerable shadow of Bobby Orr, but he still captured five Norris Trophies, given annually to the NHL's best defenseman, and is the league's record-holder for most career goals, assists, and points by a defenseman. He also served as the Bruins' team captain longer than anyone in history.

Unlike some of the other superstar defensemen in this group, Bourque never got to lift the Stanley Cup during his Bruins career (that honor came in his final season, after being traded to Colorado). But that can hardly be laid at Bourque's feet, since for most of his 20-plus seasons in Boston, he was the franchise's best player.

Phil Esposito (1967–1975)

Though Esposito's time with the Bruins was relatively short, it was in Boston that he established himself as one of the game's greatest all-time scorers. In an era in which scoring 50 goals in a season was considered elite, Esposito set a single-season mark with 76 goals. He became the prototype of the modern center, stationing himself bravely in front of the net and absorbing abuse from goaltenders and defenseman alike in exchange for the opportunity to score.

Unlike celebrated goal scorers such as Bobby Hull or Maurice Richard—who earned the nicknames "Golden Jet" and "Rocket," respectively—Esposito wasn't flashy. He was, however, unstoppable.

"Moving him," noted All-Star defenseman Brad Park, who would eventually be dealt for Esposito, "was like moving 220 pounds of dog dirt."

▶ Phil Esposito

Bobby Orr (1966–1976)

The best athletes—the true immortals—do more than set records and win championships. They do more than inspire both awe and countless imitators.

They transcend the games they play, and change them forever.

That's what Bobby Orr did for hockey.

Until Orr, a defenseman's primary role was to protect his own end of the ice, content to keep pucks out of his own net. But Orr saw—and played—the game differently. Beyond the responsibilities he had in his own end, Orr led the attack on offense, transitioning on the ice the way a skilled point guard might on the basketball court.

It made little sense to him to merely clear the puck away or pass it to some streaking teammate when he already had possession of it. Why not skate with the puck himself, darting around opponents, zipping past flat-footed defensemen?

The best defense, after all, was a good offense. Orr figured out that equation for himself, and then put it into action in a way that no one had done before.

Eddie Shore (1926–1940)

Shore began the tradition of standout defenseman for the Bruins franchise and could arguably claim to be the NHL's first superstar. The 5'11", 190-pound Shore won four Hart Trophies (league MVP), a number surpassed in league history only by Gordie Howe and Wayne Gretzky.

In addition to his legendary mean streak, Shore's toughness was matched only by his ability to control the game from his end of the ice. Opposing forwards carrying the puck into the Bruins' zone needed to have their heads up at all times to be on the lookout for his punishing hits and more-than-occasional cross-checks.

As ornery and dominant as he could be in his own end, however, Shore also was decades ahead of the likes of Orr as an offensive threat from the blue line. Five times, he reached double figures in goals scored, an unthinkable achievement for defensemen in the NHL's early years.

BOSTON BRUINS
BEST OF THE REST

Patrice Bergeron (2003–)

Bergeron might not win any scoring titles, but the centerman is the epitome of a complete player: smart, fundamentally sound, a master in the faceoff circle, and tough to play against, resulting in multiple Selke Awards, given annually to the league's best defensive forward.

Frankie Brimsek (1939–1949)

When your nickname as a goalie is "Mr. Zero," you know you've had an incredible career. One of the NHL's first American-born stars, he won the Calder Trophy (best rookie) and two Vezina Trophies. His career records for most wins and shutouts stood for more than 50 years.

Johnny Bucyk (1957–1978)

Bucyk's career with the Bruins spanned 21 seasons and nearly touched parts of three decades. He wore the "C" on his sweater as team captain, and when he retired in 1978, he was fourth on the NHL's all-time points list. He's still the Bruins' all-time leader in goals scored and second only to Ray Bourque in points.

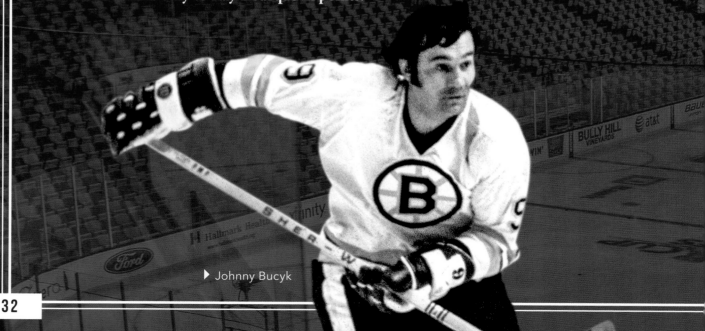

▶ Johnny Bucyk

Zdeno Chara (2006–)

At 6'9", Chara is not only the tallest player in NHL history but also a giant in terms of talent. An imposing physical presence, the Czechoslovakia-born defenseman won a Norris Trophy in 2008–09 and was a finalist several other times. He owns the game's hardest shot and captained the Bruins to the 2011 Stanley Cup, their first in almost four decades.

Aubrey "Dit" Clapper (1927–1947)

Clapper was both dominant and versatile, making the All-Star team both as a defenseman and as a forward. A key part of three Stanley Cup championship teams—a feat unmatched by any other Bruins player—he's also a Hockey Hall of Fame inductee.

Bill Cowley (1935–1947)

At a time when goal-scoring was at a premium, Cowley had one season in which he averaged nearly two points per game. He won the Hart Trophy as the league MVP twice and retired as the NHL's leading scorer.

Cam Neely (1986–1996)

Neely helped define the position of power forward, combining brute strength and goal-scoring ability. He scored 50 goals three times, including one season in which he reached the magical mark in just 44 games. After a career cut short by a knee injury, he later became team president.

Milt Schmidt (1936–1955)

Schmidt was a Bruins lifer and remains the only person in franchise history to serve the club as player, coach, and general manager. As a player, the perennial All-Star was the league's fourth all-time scorer when he retired and was third in assists. In the front office his landmark trades helped lay the foundation for two Stanley Cup–winning teams.

Tiny Thompson (1928–1938)

Arguably the greatest goalie in franchise history, Thompson still holds Bruins career records for games played in goal, shutouts, wins, and goals-against average. He won four Vezina Trophies and helped lead Boston to the Stanley Cup in 1929.

CHAPTER 2
THE
CELTICS

In the domain of some sports, it was the poor fortune of many Boston fans to watch their most bitter rivals realize dynastic success, to become synonymous with winning.

Red Sox fans had to endure the habitual winning of the New York Yankees. It was the same in hockey: The Bruins wandered through the NHL's desert, endlessly in search of a Stanley Cup, only to have the dreaded Montreal Canadiens win with alarming regularity. For all of this heartbreak, however, Boston sports fans had an antidote: the Celtics.

For every Bucky Dent home run, for every Bill Buckner misplay, for every "too many men on the ice," for every phantom "roughing the passer" call, there were the Celtics, symbolized by the giddy leprechaun, and a vivid reminder that championships weren't always won by the other guys.

Boston could win, too. And the Celtics did that at an unparalleled rate.

◀ Paul Pierce celebrates the Celtics' 17th NBA title after beating the Lakers in 2008.

CORNERSTONES Bill Russell and Red Auerbach guided the Celtics to the greatest dynasty in US professional sports.

Founded in 1946, the Celtics won almost one-quarter of all NBA titles from their inception through 2017. From the late 1950s through the end of the 1960s, they featured the league's winningest coach in Red Auerbach and player in Bill Russell. They won at a rate that has never been equaled, never mind surpassed.

And after a brief down period, the franchise was revitalized twice—once led by Larry Bird, and later by a dominant trio known affectionately as "the Big Three." Measured as a percentage of seasons played and championships captured, the Celtics are, quite simply, the most successful franchise in North America's four major sports.

The Dynasty

Founded by Walter Brown in 1946, the Celtics struggled to survive—a not uncommon fate for many teams in the fledging Basketball Association of America. Brown didn't have a background in basketball; he was a hockey man. But he knew enough to know what he didn't know, and in 1950 he hired the perfect coach to make the basketball decisions for him.

Arnold "Red" Auerbach had built a reputation as an innovative coach and brilliant strategist with the pro teams in Washington, DC, and the Tri-Cities (in Illinois and Iowa), but he had also clashed with owners at both stops. In Boston, Brown gave Auerbach nearly total authority—and then did the smart thing by getting out of the way.

Auerbach was more than the coach, of course. He was the de facto GM, assembling the roster as he saw fit. But he was so much more than either of those roles. In the league's early days, Auerbach was the traveling secretary, director of marketing, and business manager—all at once.

What he did best, however, was construct and then guide a team. Through shrewd dealing and negotiating, a remarkable prescience, and some leprechaun-generated good luck, Auerbach began assembling the franchise's first dynasty.

The Celtics built a solid core behind the likes of point guard Bob Cousy and shooting guard Bill Sharman. Then 1956 happened. In the draft, Auerbach selected two more future Hall of Famers in forward Tommy Heinsohn and point guard K.C. Jones. Those two alone would have constituted one of the better draft classes in league history. But in the big picture Heinsohn and Jones, great as they were, were nearly afterthoughts compared with a draft-day trade that sent second overall pick Bill Russell to the Celtics.

With that foundation in place, the franchise was off and running. In 1957, the Celtics captured their first title by beating the St. Louis Hawks 125–123 in double overtime in Game 7 of the NBA Finals. Rookies Russell and Heinsohn led the way, with Russell snaring 32 rebounds while Heinsohn poured in 37 points.

It was the start of an incredible run. The Celtics of the late 1950s through the late '60s won as no North American pro team had won, before or since. Starting in 1959, they won eight straight championships and 10 in 11 years. And they won with almost stunning regularity, with the consistency of a metronome. In fact, it became news when they didn't win, and even then, they came close. In the two seasons between 1956–57 and 1968–69 that the Celts weren't NBA champions, they lost in the conference finals one of those years and in the NBA Finals the other.

Beyond their championship reign, they established themselves as innovators. Auerbach effectively invented the notion of fast-break basketball, a variation of which continues to the present day. His Celtics mastered the notion of teamwork, too, leaving the role of leading scorer to opponents such as center Wilt Chamberlain, who achieved personal glory in the stat column with three teams but was beaten four times in the Finals, twice by the team-oriented Celtics.

HONDO While Bill Russell commanded the low post, John Havlicek was a stud on the outside on eight championship teams.

Instead, the Celtics emphasized ball movement, positioning, smothering defense, and a quick pace up and down the court. They became the first franchise to emphasize the importance of a "sixth man" off the bench, to keep starters fresh and maintain their frenetic tempo. The more energy the five players on the court had, the more difficult it was for the opposition to keep up.

From player rotation to their style of play, the Celtics were innovators. But what really separated them from other franchises was their success.

"The Boston Celtics," Auerbach himself once intoned, "are not a basketball team. They're a way of life."

THE FIVE BEST TRADES IN
CELTICS HISTORY

Thanks largely to Red Auerbach's unique ability to identify undervalued talent elsewhere, the Celts have acquired a surprisingly high number of key players through trade.

5. Al Jefferson, Ryan Gomes, Gerald Green, Sebastian Telfair, Theo Ratliff, and two first-round draft picks to Minnesota for Kevin Garnett (July 31, 2007)

Never before had a team given up so many players to get one player in return, but the Celtics weren't sorry. With Garnett joining Ray Allen and Paul Pierce, the Celtics won one championship (2008) and just missed another, losing in seven games to the Lakers (2010).

4. Rick Robey and two second-round draft picks to Phoenix for Dennis Johnson and first- and third-round draft picks (June 27, 1983)

The Celtics had won in 1981, but landing Johnson gave them a stalwart defender in the backcourt. DJ helped the Celts win two more championships in the 1980s.

3. The rights to Charlie Scott to Phoenix for Paul Silas (March 14, 1972)

Silas gave the Celts a stout defender and aggressive rebounder to help undersized center Dave Cowens up front. Silas won two rings with the Celts—in 1974 and 1976—before being shipped to Denver as part of a three-team trade.

2. Two draft picks (Nos. 1 and 13) to Golden State for Robert Parish and the No. 3 pick (June 9, 1980)

It's considered a good trade when you can get not one but two Hall of Famers in one move. Parish and Kevin McHale, whom the Celtics selected with the draft pick, filled out the frontcourt with Larry Bird and pointed the Celts to three championships.

1. Ed McCauley and Cliff Hagan to the St. Louis Hawks for Bill Russell (April 30, 1956)

Any and all lists of greatest Celtics trades start here. St. Louis picked University of San Francisco center Bill Russell second overall and sent him on to the Celtics later that day. Though McCauley and Hagan were future Hall of Famers, Russell went on to become the biggest winner in North American team sports, bringing home 11 NBA championships in 13 seasons with the Celtics.

Pioneers

If *all* the Celtics did was win, that would be enough to cement their place not just as basketball's greatest franchise, but also among the world's most successful franchises, regardless of the sport. But the Celtics did so much more than win. They broke barriers, became trailblazers, and set an example for inclusion.

In assembling the dynasty that would go on to win 11 championships in 13 seasons, the Celts became the first team to integrate when they selected Chuck Cooper out of Duquesne in the second round of the 1950 draft. The team took heat for the pick, with one rival owner challenging Celtics owner Walter Brown.

"Don't you know he's a colored boy?"

Retorted Brown: "I don't care if he's striped or plaid or polka dot."

Cooper wasn't hailed as any sort of pioneer, even though baseball had integrated only three seasons earlier. Part of this was due to the relatively small profile the NBA had at the time. With franchises in places like Syracuse, New York, and Fort Wayne, Indiana, the league was far from big time, and its advances in integration received far less attention than the 1947 arrivals of Jackie Robinson and Larry Doby to organized baseball.

Perhaps in part because the NBA didn't command the spotlight, Cooper endured some rough experiences along the way. In one instance, the Celtics played some exhibition games south of the Mason-Dixon line. Cooper, not allowed to stay with his teammates at the segregated hotels, was forced to finish the game and then board a northbound train in order to find a place to spend the night. (To his everlasting credit, Bob Cousy accompanied Cooper on at least one of these treks in a show of solidarity.)

In truth, Cooper's career with the Celts was relatively nondescript. He left before the franchise won its first championship. But as he left, a host of black players replaced him on the roster, led by Bill Russell and Sam Jones.

As the franchise piled up trophy after trophy, the team integrated more fully. In 1964, the Celts made history again when they fielded a team consisting of five black starters: Russell, Sam and K.C. Jones, Tom "Satch" Sanders, and Willie Naulls. Today, such lineups are commonplace in a league in which nearly 80 percent of the players are African-American. But in the 1960s, it was groundbreaking and a point of distinction for the franchise.

"Five black men," said K.C. Jones with undisguised pride. "We were all proud of that."

In 1966, the Celtics would make history again when Auerbach retired and turned the coaching reins over to Russell, who while still playing also became the league's first black coach. (It would be another nine years before baseball had a manager of color and, incredibly, another two decades before the NFL hired its first black head coach.)

Sadly, as the Celtics were breaking down barriers as an organization, some of their players were themselves the victims of racism in their own city. Occasionally, racial taunting of the home team took place in the Garden, and Russell's home in a nearby suburb was once vandalized, with the perpetrator defecating in the center's bed.

Russell wasn't shy about reacting to incidents of injustice, and to some he came off as openly hostile to white people. Although he claimed to be misquoted in a magazine article that quoted him saying, "I hate all white people," Russell wasn't one to avoid the sensitive topic of race. He knew his celebrity gave him a bully pulpit from which to speak. And he further recognized that his celebrity was a double-edged sword.

"I'm acceptable most places as somebody's guest because I'm Bill Russell, pro basketball player," he once said. "But in many of those same places, I wouldn't be acceptable as Bill Russell, US citizen."

Further driving home the inequities was the knowledge that the Celtics, one of sport's greatest dynasties, were badly outdrawn in their own building by the cellar-dwelling Bruins. It's impossible in hindsight to determine how much of this was driven by race. Was hockey more

▲ K.C. Jones won eight NBA titles as a player with the Celtics and added two more as a head coach.

popular because the players were all white? Were fans more comfortable identifying with players whom they resembled? Or was hockey merely more popular in New England?

Whatever the narrative, the Celtics didn't seem overly concerned. They were too busy winning—and, not incidentally, making history along the way—to care.

Rivals: The Lakers

In sports, greatness needs a reflection, someone against whom you can be measured. Muhammad Ali had Joe Frazier, and their three fights came not only to define the two boxers but to elevate them. While Ali had memorable bouts with Sonny Liston and later George Foreman, it was Frazier with whom he would always be linked. Ali could not have been The Greatest without a worthy opponent.

In the NBA, the Celtics became the league's first superteam during the 1950s and 1960s. But beyond the opponents in secondary cities (Syracuse, Rochester, Fort Wayne), the Celts needed a worthy opponent against whom they could be matched, another team that boasted of stars and could claim its own history of success.

In short, they needed a true rival. And in the Los Angeles Lakers, they found one.

Did they ever.

The rivalry spanned several eras. The first great dynasty began in Minneapolis, where the Lakers—their nickname making far more sense in the Land of 10,000 Lakes than in arid Southern California—won the 1949 Basketball Association of America championship and then took four of the first five NBA titles after the league was formed in 1949–50.

But just as the Lakers were about to make their way westward to Los Angeles, the balance in the league underwent a seismic shift, too. The Celtics began their unprecedented run in 1956–57 with their NBA Finals win over the St. Louis Hawks for banner No. 1. From there the Celts went on to win 11 championships in 13 seasons, a period during which a Celtics-Lakers Finals became almost habitual. From 1958–59 through the end of the Celts' dynastic run in 1968–69, the two teams met with the NBA title on the line seven times, with the Celtics coming out on the winning end every time.

From 1961–62 through the end of the Bill Russell era in 1968–69, the Lakers became the Washington Generals to the Celtics' Harlem Globetrotters. Regardless of personnel or coaching changes, the result seemed almost preordained.

In a now-legendary episode, Lakers owner Jack Kent Cooke filled the rafters of his Fabulous Forum in Inglewood, California, with celebratory balloons meant to be released when the Lakers finally ended their run of futility and bested the Celtics in Game 7 of the 1968–69 Finals.

Predictably, this backfired in the biggest way imaginable. Red Auerbach made sure that his charges were made acutely aware of this affront and used it as pregame motivation. The result: another Celtics win, producing one more banner to hoist at the dingy Garden.

The 1970s saw the two teams take a decade off from their bitter—and to date, lopsided—rivalry. The Lakers won their first championship since moving to LA, but because they drew the New York Knicks as opponents, it didn't have the same feeling of accomplishment. The Celtics won two more titles, but those came at the expense of opponents in nouveau basketball cities— Milwaukee and Phoenix.

"It was probably the best rivalry in all of professional sports at the time."

- Byron *SCOTT*
FORMER LAKERS GUARD

As it turns out, the run of NBA Finals in the 1960s was merely an appetizer for what was to come. The 1980s saw the NBA explode in popularity, not a little of that explosion driven by the renewed rivalry between the Celts and Lakers, and personified by the matchup of Larry Bird and Magic Johnson.

The two squared off in the NCAA championship game in March 1979, and six months later they joined their respective NBA teams. Soon, both had helped their franchises back to glory. The Lakers improved by 13 games in the standings, while the Celtics more than doubled their win total from the previous season.

The teams would not only be inexorably linked but also come to dominate the league. Consider: either the Celtics or the Lakers reached the NBA Finals in every year of the decade, with the teams combining for eight titles—three for the Celtics and five for the Lakers. Throughout the 1980s, it was as though the two teams blotted out the sun. No other teams mattered. The NBA orbited around Bird and Magic and their supporting casts.

Sadly, race entered the equation somewhat. Led by three star white players (Bird, Kevin McHale, and Danny Ainge), the Celts were portrayed—both nationally and locally—as "smart," "traditional," and "cerebral," while the Lakers, led by black stars (Magic, Kareem Abdul-Jabbar, and James Worthy), were "flashy" and "athletic," with a "playground" sensibility. None of the code words, however, could detract from the competition. This was basketball as art, played at the highest level—with a mixture of animosity and respect.

"It was probably the best rivalry in all of professional sports at the time," recalled former Lakers guard Byron Scott. "You're talking about two of the best franchises (of all time)."

Intensity apart, there was an aesthetic element to the games, along with a staggering amount of talent. In the three Finals meetings in the 1980s—in 1984, 1985, and 1987—a total of 10 Hall of Famers participated.

However, Bird's 1992 retirement, and the death of Reggie Lewis the next summer, led to a rare fallow period in the franchise's history—and in the rivalry. From 1993–94 through 2000–01, the Celtics reached the playoffs just once as the team fell into the NBA nether world of the salary cap era—

▲ Larry Bird shoots over Kareem Abdul-Jabbar in a 1984 game.

neither good enough to contend for a championship nor bad enough to warrant a lottery pick. This era included the franchise's disastrous 1997 decision to hire Rick Pitino and grant him complete control over all basketball matters. Not until Pitino left in 2001 did the Celtics begin to approach respectability. Alas, the Lakers could hardly relate: LA was in the midst of its three-peat of championships with Kobe Bryant and Shaquille O'Neal.

Finally, in the summer of 2007, things in Boston began to change dramatically. The turnaround was sparked by a series of bold moves by Danny Ainge, by now the general manager. Ainge, who had been part of two Celtics championships in the 1980s as a player, seemed to be channeling the late, great Red Auerbach when he obtained smooth-shooting Ray Allen from Seattle. A little more than a month later, he engineered a massive trade with

THE FIVE GREATEST GAMES IN
CELTICS HISTORY

A list of great Celtics games could fill a book by itself. These five games rise above the rest.

5. "Havlicek Stole the Ball!"—Game 7, Eastern Division finals (April 15, 1965)

This game might be known more for its accompanying radio call than the game itself. It was Game 7 of the Eastern Division finals, and the Celtics clung to a one-point lead over the Philadelphia 76ers. Sixers guard Hal Greer attempted to inbound the ball, but John Havlicek stole the pass and Sam Jones dribbled out the clock. The Celts went on to win their seventh NBA title in a row, and Johnny Most's call lives on in infamy.

4. Setting the Suns—Game 5, NBA Finals (June 4, 1976)

This was the first NBA Finals game to go to triple overtime. The second overtime finished with a buzzer beater by the Suns' Gar Heard, but the Celtics prevailed in the third OT behind six points from role player Glenn McDonald. Two days later, the Celts finished off Phoenix for their 13th championship.

3. The Balloons—Game 7, NBA Finals (May 5, 1969)

Lakers owner Jack Kent Cooke was convinced that his team was finally going to beat the Celtics to win an NBA title, and he filled the rafters of the Fabulous Forum with balloons in anticipation. Bill Russell, in the final game of his remarkable career, was not going to let that happen. "Those (expletive) balloons are staying up there," Russell told the Lakers' Jerry West at the start of the game. And stay they did—Celtics 108, Lakers 106.

2. Henderson's Steal—Game 2, NBA Finals (May 31, 1984)

Showing great anticipation, point guard Gerald Henderson stole a Lakers inbounds pass with seconds remaining in overtime. His layup tied the score and sent the game into overtime, where the Celtics hung on. They would go on to win the Finals, too, and this would represent the only championship over the Lakers in three tries in the 1980s.

1. Bird vs. Dominique—Game 7, Eastern Conference finals (May 22, 1988)

This was Game 7 and an epic showdown between two sharpshooters, as Larry Bird and Atlanta's Dominique Wilkins put on a great scoring display. Wilkins finished with 47 points, but Bird scored 20 in the fourth quarter alone to carry the Celts to victory and on to the Finals.

the Minnesota Timberwolves, sending five players and two first-round draft picks for center-forward Kevin Garnett.

Together with Paul Pierce, the Celts now had a "Big Three" with whom to compete in a league that was dominated by groups of star players. In the first year the trio played together, the Celts made the single biggest improvement in NBA history, winning 42 games more than they did the previous season and capturing their 17th championship. The vanquished opponent? Why, the Lakers, of course, making the return to glory all the more sweet.

▲ It's pure pandemonium as Kevin Garnett and the Celtics bring the NBA title back to Boston in 2008.

Two years later, the Celts found their way back to the Finals, and once more they drew the Lakers as their opponent. This time, LA overcame a 3–2 series deficit and won both Game 6 and 7, erasing a 13-point third-quarter lead by the Celtics in Game 7.

The Celts were weakened by the loss of center Kendrick Perkins, whose knee injury in the first quarter of Game 6 forced him to miss the rest of the series. The team sorely missed his rebounding and inside defensive presence. Still, two trips to the Finals in the span of three years helped put a little luster back on a franchise that had weathered a 22-year dry spell. And that both were rematches with the Lakers? It's hard to complain about that, either.

BOSTON CELTICS
MOUNT RUSHMORE

Larry Bird (1979–1992)

It speaks to the greatness of this franchise that an iconic player such as Bird doesn't even qualify—by most observers, anyway—as the greatest or most important player in team history. That honor is reserved for Bill Russell. But Bird's greatness and impact are undeniable. Together with Magic Johnson—and later Isiah Thomas and Michael Jordan—he helped elevate the NBA to heights of popularity it had never known.

His effect was immediate and dramatic. In Bird's rookie season of 1979–80, he helped the Celtics *more than double* their win total from the previous season. By his second season he was leading the franchise back to glory with its first of three championships in that decade, one of five trips to the NBA Finals the Celtics made during the 1980s. On three other occasions, the Celts qualified for the NBA's final four, losing in the conference finals, just short of another trip to the winner's circle.

Bird wasn't the fastest or strongest player in the league, but those deficiencies were cleverly hidden by countless other skills. He had terrific instincts, great court awareness, and an aura of confidence about himself that would doom opponents.

"There will never," said Johnson, "be another player like Larry Bird."

Bob Cousy (1950–1963)

Cousy could lay claim to being the Celtics' first superstar, and by extension, the NBA's first, as well. In an era during which the set shot was still the preferred method of scoring, Cousy brought an undeniable flair to the court, with behind-the-back, no-look passes while essentially inventing the position of point guard.

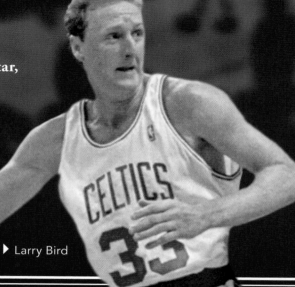

▶ Larry Bird

Undersized at 6'1", Cousy more than made up for his lack of size with a spectacular ability to see the entire floor and direct an offense. Off the court, Cousy stood in solidarity with black players who were battling bigotry and discrimination, and he later was instrumental in founding the NBA players' union. When he retired, a loudmouth fan at Boston Garden famously seized a moment of silence during the ceremony and voiced what everyone was thinking: "We love you, Cooz."

It was impossible not to.

John Havlicek (1962–1978)

For 16 seasons, Havlicek was a veritable Swiss Army knife on the basketball court for the Celts. Need a shooting guard? Havlicek could be that. How about a small forward? He could handle that, too. What about a sixth man coming off the bench? Havlicek to the rescue. There was little he couldn't—or wouldn't—do. He could score, defend, run the floor, or grab a rebound.

Havlicek was the bridge between the Russell-era dynasty and the era when the Celts began winning again, with Dave Cowens as their center, in the mid-1970s.

He was named an NBA All-Star 13 times, and yet he was more aptly known as the consummate team player, ready to adapt to whatever role was needed, while subjugating his own personal goals. Remarkably durable—he missed more than five games in a season just three times in his long career—and with the ability to rise to the occasion ("Havlicek stole the ball!"), his name rightfully belongs on a short list of the franchise's greatest players ever.

Bill Russell (1956–1969)

In 13 seasons in the NBA, Russell seldom led the league in any statistical category. Once, he led the NBA in average minutes played, and once he led the league in games played. And, yes, five times, he led the league in rebounding, but only twice after his first three seasons in the league.

That's because Russell wasn't one to be bogged down in statistics. He had bigger things in mind. Namely, winning. And William Fenton Russell did more winning than any professional basketball player ever. He played as though he needed to win the way others needed oxygen. He turned it into an art form, winning at every level—in high school, in college, as an Olympian, and mostly with the Celtics, when he won 11 titles in 13 seasons, the last two when he doubled as coach.

BOSTON CELTICS
BEST OF THE REST

Dave Cowens (1970–1980)

An undersized center at 6'8", Cowens made up for his (relative) lack of size with effort, smart positional play, and an unmatched toughness. He matched up with bigger centers (Abdul-Jabbar, Nate Thurmond, Willis Reed) and more than held his own while driving the Celts to a pair of championships in the 1970s.

Kevin Garnett (2007–2013)

Obtained in a blockbuster trade in 2007, Garnett made his presence felt immediately, helping lead the Celtics to a championship in his first season. He impacted the game as a ferocious defender, a relentless rebounder, and an adept scorer. But it was his leadership that might have meant the most as he helped end the Celts' 22-year title drought.

Tommy Heinsohn (1956–1965)

Heinsohn filled the role of power forward—before the term was popularized—for the Celtics' first dynastic run. He could score, rebound, and run the floor and was unafraid to use his size and strength. He won a championship in every season of his playing career except one. He also went on to coach the Celtics for nine seasons, winning two titles, and later served as a TV analyst on their local telecasts.

▶ Sam Jones

Sam Jones (1957–1969)

If Russell was the defensive rock in the middle around whom the great Celtics teams of the 1960s orbited, Jones was its offensive driving force, scoring as a point guard,

off guard or small forward. When those dynastic teams needed a big bucket, they more often than not got it from Jones, who gained a well-earned reputation for being a clutch performer on the biggest of stages.

Kevin McHale (1980–1993)

McHale would forever be in the shadow of Larry Bird, but he possessed an unmatched inside game with great post moves. McHale could score, he could rebound, and as Kurt Rambis of the Los Angeles Lakers discovered in the 1984 Finals, he could dish out a clothesline to send a physical message. Whether he was coming off the bench as the team's sixth man or starting up front, McHale always had an impact. A seven-time All-Star and three-time champion, he helped redefine the power forward position.

Robert Parish (1980–1994)

Parish never got the recognition afforded other centers. He wasn't Kareem Abdul-Jabbar or Hakeem Olajuwon, but he was the perfect fit for those great Celtics teams, able to score inside and outside, run the floor, and start the break with his work on the boards.

Paul Pierce (1998–2013)

Pierce was a silky-smooth scorer whose misfortune it was to be a Celtic largely at a time when the franchise was going through a fallow period. Pierce was an offensive machine who could beat teams off the dribble or with a jumper and averaged nearly 22 points during his 15-year stay with the Celts, which did include one title.

Jo Jo White (1969–1979)

A member of the Basketball Hall of Fame, White was a standout two-way guard over nine-plus seasons in Boston, averaging 18.4 points per game and earning a reputation as a deadly (and clutch) shooter. He was an integral piece to two championship teams and incredibly durable, going more than five seasons without missing a game.

CHAPTER 3

THE PATRIOTS

From the humblest of beginnings, the New England Patriots have become football's most dominant team in the 21st century.

Launched in 1960 for a $25,000 franchise fee—with much of that money borrowed—the Patriots were once no one's idea of a model franchise. For their first decade of existence as charter members of the American Football League, the Boston Patriots gave new meaning to the word nomadic. They played home games at Fenway Park and at three Boston-area colleges: Boston University, Boston College, and Harvard. Once, they even played a "home" game in Birmingham, Alabama.

The franchise was run on a shoestring budget. When they traveled to one road game in the early 1960s, the players were instructed not to turn down the bedding in their hotel rooms so the team could qualify for a discounted rate.

◀ The Patriots had a long way to go before Tom Brady began leading the way to championships in the 2000s.

In 1971, the Patriots settled in the Boston suburb of Foxborough, finally having a stadium to call their own. Yet even the new stadium got off to a rough start, with the Schaefer Stadium toilets exploding on opening night and a traffic jam on the only access road to the stadium resulting in fans being stuck for hours and hours.

And that was just the off-the-field craziness. The football wasn't any better. Throughout the 1960s, the Patriots were mediocre. During that first decade they reached the postseason exactly once, and that ended with a humiliating 51–10 loss to the San Diego Chargers in the 1963 AFL Championship Game.

In the post-merger era, with the NFL fully absorbing the AFL in 1970, the Pats got back to the playoffs for the first time in 1976. Two years later they won their first division title, but in the final weeks of the season coach Chuck Fairbanks was found to have cut a deal to become coach at the University of Colorado, resulting in his suspension by team owner Billy Sullivan.

This sort of amateurish behavior marked the team for much of its first few decades. The Patriots were always, it seemed, on the run—from stadium to stadium, from representing "Boston" to briefly "Bay State" to finally "New England." They churned through coaches. And always there was the ineptitude on the field. In their first 16 years, the Patriots had just five winning seasons. Then, after a decade in which they attained respectability, they slid downhill again.

The team went through three owners in 14 years. At various points the Pats were rumored to be headed everywhere from Hartford to St. Louis, or from Tampa to Seattle. They found themselves embroiled in a massive sexual harassment suit for their treatment of

NUMBER ONE No quarterback has won more Super Bowls than Tom Brady.

a female reporter in their locker room. Even their first two trips to the Super Bowl, after the 1985 and 1996 seasons, ended in lopsided defeats.

For periods of both the 1980s and early 1990s, they were the rare NFL franchise that couldn't sell out its home games, subjecting New England to television blackouts. There were player holdouts, demands to be traded, and a revolving door of coaches and quarterbacks. The Patriots were, in short, a laughingstock.

Finally, in the mid-1990s, the team's ownership situation stabilized and, with it, so did the franchise. In March 2000, the Patriots began construction on a (mostly) privately funded state-of-the-art stadium. Bill Belichick arrived that same year. Before long, the same franchise that had bumbled and stumbled through much of its first 40 years of existence became the benchmark for football excellence.

From their inception to 1993, the Patriots had a .450 winning percentage. From 1989 to 1993, they bottomed out on the field, going a lowly 19–61. Since then, though, the Patriots have been dominant. From 1994 through 2017, they won nearly 70 percent of their games and went to nine Super Bowls, winning five of them.

Of course, the Patriots being the Patriots, controversy never fully left. Under Belichick, the team faced disciplinary action for filming other teams' signals and later for having failed to inflate footballs to their prescribed weight. Despite that, the Patriots have become the NFL's gold standard, a prospect that would have been laughable as recently as 2000.

Growing Pains

Some football franchises date back decades and claim multigenerational ownership from the same established families. The Rooneys continue to own the Pittsburgh Steelers. The same goes for the Maras and the New York Giants. The link between some families and franchises, in fact, is so strong that one, the Cleveland Browns, is named after the original owner.

The same cannot be said for the Patriots.

In the past, NFL owners were often wealthy "sportsmen" who viewed team ownership as a civic commitment or their teams as expensive playthings. Billy Sullivan didn't fit the stereotype. Sullivan was a former Boston-area sportswriter, publicist, and salesman who was awarded the eighth and final franchise of the fledgling AFL only after he cobbled together some loans and came up with the $25,000 franchise fee necessary to join the league.

Other AFL owners at the time included Texas oilman Lamar Hunt and New York entertainment lawyer Sonny Werblin. Sullivan was nowhere near their financial class. For one thing, he had no playing facility to call his own. So the Patriots, in their first decade of existence, changed stadiums with alarming frequency.

Finally, in 1971 they settled in Foxborough—or Foxboro, in local parlance—about 30 miles southwest of Boston and 20 miles northeast of Providence, Rhode Island. The team built a 60,000-seat stadium that was almost primitive—a concrete bowl with aluminum bleacher seats. It wasn't much, but it was theirs, and it would remain their home for 30 years. But amid all the upheaval associated with the franchise, one constant remained: bad football.

During the AFL years the Patriots didn't have the resources to compete with the more established NFL for star players coming out of college. To convince marquee names like Joe Namath to pass on the NFL in favor of the AFL cost money, and the Pats didn't have it. What they had were retreads, journeymen, small-college players, and those not quite good enough to play in the NFL. And the results were predictable.

Although the Pats were surprisingly competitive on the field in the first few seasons, even reaching the AFL Championship Game in 1963, they soon entered a phase, from 1965 to 1975, during which they recorded just one winning season.

The franchise was a comedy of errors, some funnier than others. When they introduced Clive Rush as the team's third head coach in 1969, Rush was nearly electrocuted as he grabbed the microphone at the press conference.

On another occasion, running back Bob Gladieux, having been cut by the team days before the season opener, was watching a game from the stands at Harvard Stadium. When Gladieux's friend headed to the concession stands for a couple of pregame beers, Gladieux heard himself being paged on the stadium public-address system. He reported to the locker room, was told that the Pats were unexpectedly short a player, and signed a contract anew. Minutes later, he was part of the kickoff coverage team. His friend, meanwhile, had returned to his seat, wondering about his friend's whereabouts. Soon, he learned.

"Tackle made by Bob Gladieux," came the announcement.

HOME SWEET HOME After some false starts, the Patriots in 1971 established their home southwest of Boston in Foxborough, Massachusetts.

There were other examples of the franchise's tragicomic existence. At Alumni Stadium, permanent home of Boston College and temporary home of the Patriots, a fire engulfed a section of the stands. In self-preservation, hundreds of fans poured onto the field while play continued at the other end.

On another occasion, during the 1971 offseason, the team traded for talented-but-troubled running back Duane Thomas from the Dallas Cowboys. In his first practice with the team, Thomas resolutely refused a coach's direction to assume a three-point stance and walked off the field in protest. The trade was soon rescinded.

These sorts of anecdotes dot Patriots history. With the benefit of hindsight, they appear charming, though at the time, they defined the franchise's ineptitude. Most of all they in no way predicted the sort of dynastic franchise into which the Patriots would eventually morph.

THE FIVE GREATEST GAMES IN
PATRIOTS HISTORY

From nomadic cellar-dwellers to a 21st century dynasty, the Patriots have had a colorful—and varied—history. Here are their greatest games, with, naturally, more focus on the Glory Years.

5. Taming the Dolphins—AFC Championship Game (January 12, 1986)

For the Patriots, the Orange Bowl was their own House of Horrors. Heading into this matchup, the Pats had lost 18 consecutive games to the host Miami Dolphins. But with a trip to the Super Bowl at stake, the Pats pulled off a convincing 31–14 victory.

4. The "Tuck Rule" Game—AFC Championship Game (January 19, 2002)

An obscure rule played a huge role in this divisional playoff game win over the Oakland Raiders. Instead of a fumble, the officials determined that quarterback Tom Brady meant to "tuck" the ball into his body, and the Pats retained possession at a key point in the fourth quarter. That led to a game-tying field goal, a winning field goal in overtime, and, eventually, their first Super Bowl win.

3. Malcolm Butler's Miracle—Super Bowl XLIX (February 1, 2015)

The Pats seemed headed for certain defeat as the Seattle Seahawks drove toward their goal line in the final minute. But Malcolm Butler's interception at the 1-yard line saved the game and gave the Pats their fourth ring.

2. Brady's Comeback—Super Bowl LI (February 5, 2017)

The Patriots, trailing the Atlanta Falcons 28–3 in the third quarter, engineered the greatest comeback in Super Bowl—heck, maybe in football—history and scored 31 unanswered points to win 34–28 in overtime.

1. Champions at Last—Super Bowl XXXVI (February 3, 2002)

The first one is always the sweetest—and the most memorable. The Patriots were massive underdogs against the high-scoring St. Louis Rams, but Brady wrapped up his dream season by leading the Patriots to the franchise's first championship. An Adam Vinatieri field goal in the closing seconds sealed it.

Will They Stay, or Will They Go?

On a number of occasions, New England nearly lost its pro football team. It's safe to say that there were times when few would have cared, or even noticed.

For their first decade of existence, the Patriots were vagabonds. It wasn't until their 12th season that they had a stadium to call their own, and before the stadium was hastily constructed in 1971, the Pats were rumored to be headed to Tampa or Seattle.

That air of instability hung above the team even after it settled in Foxborough. While other franchises were wildly profitable and played in front of sellout crowds, the Patriots often had half-empty houses and economic uncertainty.

In the late 1980s, things bottomed out. The Sullivan family, which had owned the team since its inception and was never flush with cash the way some other NFL scions were, found itself in dire financial straits after a disastrous involvement with Michael Jackson's Victory Tour in 1984. The concert tour, with Chuck Sullivan, Billy's eldest son, serving as promoter, was a flop, and the losses soon amounted to more than the value of the team and the antiquated stadium in which it played.

Not everything was dismal during this time. In 1985, the Patriots built momentum over the second half of the season and, winning three straight playoff games on the road, made their first Super Bowl appearance. It was there, however, that the sad-sack Pats reared their ugly heads again. The team was on the losing end of what was then the most lopsided

Super Bowl in history, losing to the Chicago Bears 46–10. The day after the defeat, news broke that tied the Patriots to a massive drug scandal.

Simply put, the Sullivans' time to sell had come. To their credit, the family sought local ownership with a commitment to remain in Foxborough. In Victor Kiam, they found just that. Kiam—the owner of Remington Products, makers of electric shavers—purchased the Patriots for $85 million in 1988. However, four years later, finding himself in debt and embroiled in controversy following a 1990 incident involving Patriots players and a female *Herald* reporter, Kiam sold controlling interest in the team to James Busch Orthwein.

Orthwein, a St. Louis businessman, had made no secret that he was in search of a football franchise for his own hometown—one to replace the Cardinals, who had left for Phoenix in 1988. And sure enough, he took steps to move the Patriots to St. Louis, but he found his path blocked. At about the time that the team itself had been sold to Kiam, the stadium had been sold for $22 million to Robert Kraft, who owned an adjacent racetrack. Under Kraft the stadium had a lease that ran through 2001.

When Kraft enforced his stadium lease, Orthwein's escape path to St. Louis was blocked. Because he had only bought the franchise in order to move it, Orthwein had no interest in remaining owner and sold the team to Kraft in 1994.

Kraft was a Boston-area native who had been a Pats season-ticket holder since the first season in Foxborough. He had sat in traffic jams on Route 1, walked a mile or more from the adjacent parking lots, and sat uncomfortably on the stadium's aluminum bleachers, which were either sizzling in the late-summer heat or freezing in the cold of December.

Kraft was a Patriots fan, and though more wealthy than most, he understood firsthand how the fan base's loyalty had been tested over the years. He, too, had witnessed the ownership changes that threatened the team's future. He had personally watched the dismal product on the field and had suffered in the substandard stadium.

His arrival meant that, for the first time in six years, the team and its rickety stadium were owned by the same party. And he soon set out to replace dilapidated Foxboro Stadium (as it was then called, its third name).

▲ Bob Kraft brought new optimism to Patriots fans when he bought the team in 1994.

Kraft explored sites in South Boston, in other suburban areas, and even in nearby Rhode Island. The problem was securing public financing. While other cities were in the habit of providing hundreds of millions of dollars to help teams construct new stadiums, the political climate in Boston was different. Political leaders saw these subsidies as an example of corporate welfare, and with state debt piling up, such handouts weren't viable.

Finally, Kraft thought he had a deal with the Massachusetts legislature to provide $72 million in infrastructure aid if Kraft pledged to privately finance the stadium's construction. But when the House of Representatives backed out, Kraft felt he had no recourse but to look for alternatives outside of Massachusetts.

In 1998, he found one, a sweetheart deal in Connecticut. Governor John Rowland, desperate to make up for the loss of the NHL's Whalers a year earlier and intent on revitalizing downtown Hartford, proposed a new stadium to be built with 100 percent public money.

Kraft appeared at a signing ceremony that included plans for the Pats to move to Hartford in time for the 2001 season. The league wasn't happy about sacrificing the No. 6 TV market (Boston) in exchange for one that didn't crack the top 30. And even with the state's largesse, Kraft seemed to regard the agreement as bittersweet—at the ceremony, as Rowland and other Connecticut officials beamed, Kraft had tears in his eyes. They did not appear to be tears of joy.

Fate soon interceded, however. The proposed site—known as Adriaen's Landing—was found to be polluted, delaying site preparation and pushing back the proposed date of completion. This provided the state of Massachusetts with a second chance. With the help of league officials, led by NFL Chief Operating Officer Roger Goodell (oh, the irony), the Massachusetts legislature agreed to contribute about $70 million for infrastructure.

The Patriots would stay after all in a new, state-of-the-art facility, Gillette Stadium, which opened in 2002. And they would reign, adding five championship banners in their first 14 seasons there.

Everything Changes

In the span of just three months in early 2000, two events took place that would change the path of the New England Patriots and alter the history of the NFL forever.

Not that anyone could have projected that at the time.

First, Bill Belichick abruptly resigned as coach of the New York Jets to take the same position with the Patriots. Then the Patriots used their sixth-round draft pick to select quarterback Tom Brady from the University of Michigan.

At the time, neither move seemed particularly earth-shattering. Brady was an afterthought—as many other 199th picks before and after him would be. As for Belichick, he hardly seemed to have the stuff to turn around a woebegone franchise, much less win multiple Super Bowls. His reputation at the time was that of an innovative defensive mind best suited as a coordinator. After all, he had seemed entirely over his head during his one previous head coaching opportunity in Cleveland.

Under Belichick, the Browns had gone 36–44 in five seasons with but one playoff win (over, of all teams, the Patriots). Along the way, Belichick managed to offend or disappoint everyone in his path. He feuded with the media. He benched uber-popular quarterback Bernie Kosar. His game plans and schemes seemed unimaginative. The end of his tenure coincided with the franchise's planned move from Cleveland to Baltimore. Were it not for despised owner Art Modell, Belichick might have been even more reviled.

Belichick made a one-year pit stop with the Patriots in 1996, coaching the defensive backfield, and then moved with Bill Parcells, his old mentor, to the Jets, for whom he served as defensive coordinator. In 2000, when Parcells moved from coach to GM, Belichick was contractually promoted as his replacement, a move that lasted about 24 hours. Unsure about the franchise's future and commitment, Belichick utilized a contractual clause to escape and move to the Patriots.

What did Bob Kraft see in this coach who had failed so miserably in his first head coaching job? Call it instinct.

"I learned a long, long, long time ago," said Jonathan Kraft, Bob's son and team president, "when my dad says his gut says something is the right decision, he's always right. He's never wrong. And so, in 2000, he's like, 'We're getting Bill Belichick. Period.' And no one agreed."

But Bob Kraft was once again right.

Then, it was Belichick's turn to be right. With little fanfare, he selected Brady, a two-year starter at Michigan, in the sixth round.

At the time, Drew Bledsoe was the Patriots' starter and remained in that position throughout 2000, when the Pats finished 5–11, and into 2001. Although Bledsoe had directed the Pats to Super Bowl XXXI in January 1997, his play—and popularity—had faded in the ensuing years. Then, in the second week of that 2001 season, Bledsoe absorbed

THE TOP FIVE
PATRIOTS BARGAIN PICKS

In the NFL, most teams get it right with their first-round picks. The trick is finding talent in the later rounds, and the Patriots have done that well. Here are five great under-the-radar finds.

5. Julian Edelman, seventh round (232nd overall), 2009

A former quarterback at Kent State, Edelman went on to become Brady's favorite slot receiver and a dynamic punt returner, setting the franchise record for most punt returns for touchdowns. His acrobatic catch in Super Bowl LI was a key to their comeback, and his touchdown catch in Super Bowl XLIX put the Pats ahead to stay.

4. Steve Grogan, fifth round (116th overall), 1975

Unlike Brady, Grogan never led the Patriots to a Super Bowl championship. But he did help lead them to their first Super Bowl appearance and spent 16 seasons with the team, earning entrance to the Patriots Hall of Fame and a spot on not one but two Patriots All-Decade teams (1970s, 1980s).

3. Tedy Bruschi, third round (86th overall), 1996

Bruschi was considered undersized, one reason he was still available in the third round. But he went on to become the anchor of the Patriots' defenses in the early 2000s, and was part of three Super Bowl championship teams, earning All-Pro honors twice.

2. Adam Vinatieri, undrafted free agent, 1996

OK, we're bending the rules here, since Vinatieri wasn't drafted at all. By the Patriots or anyone else, for that matter. But that just makes his discovery all the more amazing. Vinatieri won the Pats' first two Super Bowls with last-minute field goals. Enough said.

1. Tom Brady, sixth round (199th overall), 2000

Well, duh. Brady was the 199th pick of this draft, and at the time of his arrival he barely seemed worth mentioning. As the years went on, it became clear that this was the most fortuitous pick not only in Patriots history but also in league history. With his fifth Super Bowl ring after the 2016 season, Brady stood alone among quarterbacks.

a punishing hit by Jets linebacker Mo Lewis. It seemed like a routine tackle, but it proved to have lasting consequences for Bledsoe, Brady, and the Patriots franchise.

The hit sheared a blood vessel in Bledsoe's chest and filled his abdomen with blood. Brady took over the quarterbacking duties, and though it couldn't have been anticipated, he never relinquished them.

His first few games offered no hint of what was to come. Brady played like the inexperienced quarterback that he was, with the Pats losing to the Jets, then splitting the next two games. After four weeks, the Patriots were just 1–3.

At that point, Belichick was just 6–14 in his first 20 games directing the franchise. *What was it that Kraft had seen in him?*

Then, things began to change. Brady won four of his next five games and, ultimately, nine of the next 11 to steer the Patriots into the playoffs. By then, Bledsoe was healthy again, but despite the adage that suggested a player never loses his job to injury, Brady remained the starter.

"I didn't think it was fair," Bledsoe would say years later.

And perhaps it wasn't. But football isn't about fairness. It's about results.

The Patriots—and Brady—never looked back.

Following playoff wins over Oakland and Pittsburgh, the Patriots went into Super Bowl XXXVI as heavy underdogs against the St. Louis Rams and their high-scoring offense known as "The Greatest Show on Turf." Although New England took a 17–3 lead, the Rams scored two fourth-quarter touchdowns to tie the game with just 1:30 remaining. John Madden, the Hall of Fame coach working the telecast, suggested the Patriots run out

IT'S GOOD Adam Vinatieri kicks the game-winning field goal against the St. Louis Rams in Super Bowl XXXVI.

the clock and try to win in overtime. Belichick had other ideas. Brady directed the Pats down the field and, with five completions in the final drive, got them to the Rams' 30-yard line. Field-goal range. Adam Vinatieri's 48-yarder as time expired clinched one of the Super Bowl's biggest upsets. It also was the first time in the Super Bowl's 36-year history that the game was decided on the final play.

The upset was more than that, though. It allowed the Patriots to shed the tag of lovable losers that had been affixed to them for much of their first 42 years of existence. And, coming in the aftermath of September 11, it created a link between the team, its name, and the surge of togetherness the country was feeling after the horrific attacks.

"We're all patriots now," proclaimed Robert Kraft at the postgame celebration.

The Brady-Belichick relationship was just beginning. The tandem went on to win two more Super Bowls in the next three seasons. Two subsequent trips to the Super Bowl, however, resulted in agonizing last-minute losses to the New York Giants, with the first setback in February 2008 spoiling the Patriots' bid to become the first team to go 19–0.

But the Brady-Belichick team added two more rings in a most dramatic fashion. They stopped the Seattle Seahawks at the goal line to preserve a victory in Super Bowl XLIX in February 2015, before rebounding from a 28–3 deficit to score 31 unanswered points to edge the Atlanta Falcons in overtime in Super Bowl LI two years later. Although a trip to Super Bowl LII the next year ended in a loss to the Philadelphia Eagles, the game was notable for Brady throwing a playoff-record 505 yards at age 40. Only this time, there were no last-second heroics as a game-ending Hail Mary toward Rob Gronkowski was batted down to the turf.

"Losing sucks," Brady said afterward, a sentiment he's not often had to share.

Brady, with his good looks and penchant for dramatic comebacks, gets most of the attention, but Belichick's contributions shouldn't be minimized. After failing in Cleveland, he became a more fully formed coach in New England, unveiling defensive schemes that were so brilliant in their design that the personnel at times was almost an afterthought. His genius hasn't been limited to the defensive side of the ball, either. When he traded for mercurial wide receiver Randy Moss, who had worn out his welcome in Minnesota and Oakland, he helped create the highest-scoring offense the league had ever known in 2007.

The dual protagonists, however, have always been Belichick and Brady. Together, through 2017, they had won five Super Bowls, eight conference championships, 15 division

CAN'T STOP THEM Tom Brady and the Patriots were champions again after coming back to beat the Atlanta Falcons in Super Bowl LI.

titles, and a lifetime of admiration from Patriots fans. No other coach-quarterback pairing has been that successful. Not Lombardi-Starr. Not Noll-Bradshaw. Not Walsh-Montana.

Their success has spurred a popular parlor game among football fans: Who is more responsible for the Patriots' success?

Some point to Belichick's 18–19 record in New England in games started by someone other than Brady as evidence that the quarterback is more essential to the team's success. With Brady under center, the Pats have won 78 percent of their games.

Parsing credit, however, isn't terribly relevant. Whether it's Belichick's sideline genius, his game plans, or his coaching, or Brady's calm under fire, accuracy, or leadership on the field, this can't be argued: The two are the greatest QB-coach tandem the NFL has ever known.

NEW ENGLAND PATRIOTS
MOUNT RUSHMORE

Tom Brady (2000–)

Before Brady started a regular-season game at quarterback for the New England Patriots, 25 others had held the job, ranging from B (Bledsoe) to Z (Zolak).

None came close to Brady.

Arriving as an afterthought—he was chosen 199th overall, in the sixth round, of the 2000 draft—Brady entered the 2001 training camp ranked fourth (!) on the team's depth chart. Of course, he went on to become the team's starter and won his first Super Bowl that year. Since then, he's won more Super Bowls than any quarterback anywhere (five), taken his team to eight Super Bowl appearances, set franchise records in virtually every passing category, and established himself not only as the Patriots' greatest quarterback but, beyond that, the greatest quarterback the NFL has ever known.

John Hannah (1973–1985)

Selected by the Patriots with the first of their three first-round draft picks in 1973, Hannah, a guard, was considered the greatest player in franchise history BB (Before Brady). Though he played for some poor teams in his career, no one can doubt his dominance on the offensive line.

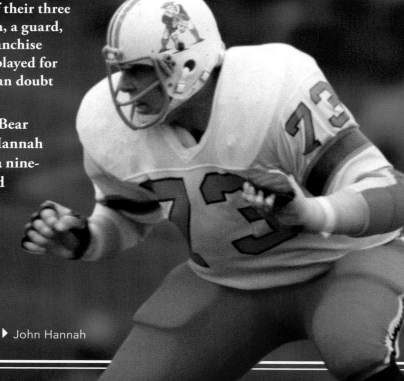

After a standout career playing for Bear Bryant at the University of Alabama, Hannah achieved stardom in the NFL. He was a nine-time Pro Bowl selection and was named to the All-Pro team every season from 1976 through 1985, his final year in the game. A 1981 *Sports Illustrated* cover story on him anointed him "The Best Offensive Lineman of All Time."

▶ John Hannah

"Hog," as he was nicknamed, was expert at both run blocking and pass protection. An All-NFL team selection in two decades (1970s and 1980s), he became the first Patriots player elected to the Pro Football Hall of Fame and was named the top guard on the NFL's 75th anniversary All-Time team.

Mike Haynes (1976–1982)

Haynes was the definition of a shutdown corner in his seven seasons with the Patriots, and if that weren't enough, he was also a fabulous kick returner. He had 28 interceptions in his seven seasons in Foxborough, and that number could have been far greater had teams not been afraid to throw in his direction. Remarkably, he was once selected to the Pro Bowl in a season in which he recorded just one interception. That honor was recognition that Haynes's mere presence in the defensive backfield was enough to dissuade opposing quarterbacks from attacking his side of the field.

In addition to Haynes's play on defense, his special teams contributions alone were staggering. He became the first Patriot in history to return a punt for a touchdown and in 1976 gained 608 yards simply from returning punts. The latter is a team record.

A contract squabble in 1982 led to him being traded, but his seven seasons were enough for him to gain election to the Patriots Hall of Fame, and his entire career was more than enough to punch his ticket to Canton.

Andre Tippett (1982–1993)

It was Tippett's misfortune to play during the same era as Lawrence Taylor. The two were similar players: athletic linebackers with an uncanny ability to disrupt offenses, and in particular, sack quarterbacks.

Tippett was athletic enough to drop back in coverage or step up to stuff the run. But what he did best was pursue the passer, as the 1980s saw the introduction of the outside linebacker as edge pass rushers. Along with Taylor, he came to define the role.

A second-round pick out of the University of Iowa, Tippett became a menace to opposing quarterbacks. He recorded 35 sacks between 1984 and 1985, a mark that stands today for the most sacks by a linebacker over a two-season span. He was named a member of the NFL All-Decade team for the 1980s, a period during which he appeared in five Pro Bowls and was twice named first team All-Pro and twice named to the second team. In 2008, he became just the second player elected to the Pro Football Hall of Fame who spent his entire career in a Patriots uniform.

NEW ENGLAND PATRIOTS
BEST OF THE REST

Bruce Armstrong (1987–2000)

Both dominant and durable (missing a total of just eight games in 14 seasons), Armstrong was a standout tackle for the Patriots. He was named to six Pro Bowls over his career and had his No. 78 jersey retired by the team. However, he might be best remembered for his twice-a-year battles with the Bills' Hall of Fame defensive end Bruce Smith.

Tedy Bruschi (1996–2008)

Bruschi was the heart and soul of the defensive teams that won the first three Super Bowls. Thought to be undersized for a linebacker upon his arrival into the league, Bruschi more than made up for that with his competitiveness and athleticism. Moreover, he also made a dramatic comeback from a stroke at age 31.

Gino Cappelletti (1960–1970)

A kicker and wide receiver, Cappelletti's career spanned the entire length of the Patriots' membership in the AFL, and he was named to the all-time All-AFL team. He was chosen as the AFL's MVP in 1964, and when he retired, he was the franchise's all-time leading scorer. He's a member of both the AFL Hall of Fame and the Patriots Hall of Fame, and many regard it as an injustice that he isn't also in the Pro Football Hall of Fame.

Ben Coates (1991–1999)

An unheralded fifth-round pick from a small college, Coates became the favorite target of quarterback Drew Bledsoe as a pass-catching right end. He was selected to both the NFL's all-decade team for the 1990s and the Patriots 50th anniversary team. Coates was named to five Pro Bowls and twice was a first-team All-Pro.

Rob Gronkowski (2010–)

Gronkowski's persona sometimes seems like a mix of pro wrestler/frat boy/overgrown kid, but there's no denying his dominance on the field. A unique blend of size, strength, and speed, he's the embodiment of the modern-day pass-catching tight end. But he's also tough and strong enough to be a menace as a blocking force. He could go down as the game's top tight end of all time, if he can stay healthy.

Ty Law (1995–2004)

If Mike Haynes is the greatest defensive back in franchise history, then Law is a close second. In his 10 seasons in Foxborough, the lights-out cornerback recorded 36 interceptions, including a league-high nine in 1998.

Stanley Morgan (1977–1989)

Morgan, a wide receiver, could stretch the field like few others. He averaged almost 20 yards per, and this came in an era before the NFL became a pass-first league. His 67 career touchdowns are still the most in team history.

Adam Vinatieri (1996–2005)

Vinatieri's last-minute kicks helped clinch the first two Super Bowl titles in team history, and his clutch kicks in other games—regular season and playoffs—could fill a book. When he left the team, he was the leading scorer in club history, and there's little doubt he will eventually be inducted into the Pro Football Hall of Fame.

Vince Wilfork (2004–2014)

Nose tackle Wilfork anchored the defensive line for 11 seasons and was part of two Super Bowl winners. Along the way he helped control the line of scrimmage and bottle things up so others—linebackers and defensive backs—could make the tackles and interceptions, and record the sacks. He made five Pro Bowls in his tenure in Foxborough.

◀ Rob Gronkowski

CHAPTER 4
THE RED SOX

As charter members of the American League, the Red Sox are one of baseball's most iconic franchises. They still play in the same ballpark they called home before World War I. They were the original franchise of both Babe Ruth and Ted Williams, two of the half-dozen most celebrated and recognizable players in the game's history. They even, for a time, won.

Early in their existence, the Red Sox (then called the Americans) captured the first World Series in 1903. From 1912 to 1918, they won four more in the span of seven seasons. And then, without warning, the winning stopped.

For a long, long time.

So much of what is identified with the Red Sox—their ballpark, their logo, their place in Boston's history, their roster of great players—was for years nearly obscured by their inability to win championships.

◀ Cy Young, now the namesake of baseball's top pitcher award, pitched for the Boston Americans, later renamed the Red Sox, from 1901 to 1908.

Like their National League cousins in futility, the Chicago Cubs, the Red Sox perfected the art of heartbreak. They did it far better, in fact, than their Windy City compatriots. The Cubs were bad, period, seldom coming close to winning. The Cubs went from 1946 through 2015 without winning a pennant. They mostly were irrelevant except for their championship drought. Cubs fans went to Wrigley Field with no expectations: They were there to soak up the sun, drink Old Style, and, almost incidentally, watch some baseball.

There was a tacit understanding between the team and its fan base: the Cubs were going to lose. No sense getting your hopes up.

Not the Red Sox. No, the Red Sox made losing an art form. They had close calls, defeats snapped from the jaws of victory, and cruel ends to their season. They teased their long-suffering fans with near misses, epic meltdowns, painful slides in the standings, and the recurring habit of losing games they seemed poised to win.

Generation after generation of Red Sox fans somehow maintained that most necessary, but ultimately dangerous, belief that someday, somehow, the Red Sox would Win It All.

And for decades, they were rewarded with nothing but disappointment.

While the Yankees won and won—26 times between the Babe Ruth trade and the year 2000—the Red Sox came to be defined by their inventive methods for failure. In 1946, 1967, 1975, and 1986, the Red Sox reached the World Series. Each time, the team forced the Series to a full seven games. Each time, the Sox lost. What's worse is that, each time, the ending was more painful than the last.

An entire cottage industry arose to chronicle their close calls and near misses. Books were written and movies produced. The team's futility was both debilitating and

"TEDDY BALLGAME" Ted Williams swings away in a 1960 game.

awe-inspiring. As Red Sox fans watched one World Series ring after another elude the team, they did so with a sense of wonder.

After a time, watching the Red Sox come up short was like watching a skilled magician working his craft: "How did they do that?"

Instead, fans came to settle for great individual performances by compelling, yet ultimately flawed, stars. Ted. Yaz. Looie. They won batting titles and Triple Crowns and led the league in homers and hits. They were larger-than-life stars who excelled during the season but always met with the same, familiar fate in October.

The historic seasons of individuals would have to suffice. But they were no substitute for the champagne-soaked celebrations of team that others—always, others—got to experience.

Finally, having run out of new ways to lose, the Red Sox won, becoming world champions in 2004. Then, like the awkward, gangly pony finally finding his footing, the winning became, if not habitual, then almost regular. They won again in 2007, and once more in 2013. After going 86 tortuous seasons without a title, the Sox improbably won three times in a decade.

For Red Sox fans of a certain age, raised on a diet of disappointment, the franchise couldn't have been recognizable. They were not, most assuredly, your father's Red Sox anymore. For their championship-starved followers, that was a very good and rewarding thing, indeed.

Stars and Heartbreaks

For long stretches of their existence, the Red Sox have come to be known for two things: iconic stars and a history of heartbreak.

Often, the stars were so big that they transcended the franchise. The Babe. Ted. Yaz. Among them, Babe Ruth even helped the Red Sox win three World Series in four seasons before being sold off to the New York Yankees in December 1919. But after that, the Sox were, for decades, most defined by a series of close calls and near misses.

Those failures weighed heavily on the stars. Ted Williams, arguably the game's greatest hitter ever, won just one pennant in a career that began in 1939 and stretched to 1960. Carl Yastrzemski, who took over left field a year after Williams retired, also had a long, remarkable career that, sadly, ended without a championship.

It's hard to determine which was a more painful part of the Red Sox history: the years when they were never a factor, doomed to also-rans and housed in the AL's basement, or the seasons when they became just competitive enough to dash their long-suffering fans' hopes. Their history includes plenty of both.

After Ruth left, the Sox went from a dynasty that had claimed five championships in 16 seasons to baseball irrelevance. Starting in 1920, their first without Ruth, the Sox endured 14 straight losing seasons.

Things began to change after Williams arrived in 1939. The Sox became respectable and then competitive. In 1946, they reached the World Series. However, with Williams nursing a bruised right elbow, the Sox fell to the St. Louis Cardinals in seven games. It was the start of an ignominious pattern.

Once a decade—except for the 1950s—the Red Sox made a habit of winning the AL pennant, facing a (slightly) better NL team in the World Series, and losing, often in the most incredible fashion, in seven games.

Worse, with each trip to the Series, the losses seemed to grow more difficult to take. With a rookie manager, Dick Williams, and a season for the ages from Yastrzemski, the 1967 Sox had gone from 100-to-1 underdogs in the spring to the most unlikely of World Series participants. In the Fall Classic, they again faced the Cardinals.

In Game 7 that October, the Sox sent their ace, Jim Lonborg, to the mound with just two days' rest. Predictably, Cardinals ace Bob Gibson outdueled Lonborg, and the Sox lost. But because the Red Sox had captivated New England with a summer-long pennant race that defied the odds, the loss to the Cards was a little easier to digest. The afterglow of that closely contested pennant race—four teams had a chance at the flag heading into the final few days—was enough to sate fans. Even the participants, years later, seemed to have made their peace with just coming close.

"I don't think this 'Impossible Dream' team would have had this same feeling if we had won everything," Lonborg would say years later. "I think the fact that we got so close and didn't win almost was a better ending than having won it all."

In 1975, the ending was all too familiar. As in 1967, the Red Sox forced a superior team—the Cincinnati Reds—to a seventh and deciding game. And, as before, Boston came up short.

This time, any bitterness associated with the loss was papered over from the afterglow of Game 6, a 12-inning affair culminating in Carlton Fisk's game-winning homer off the left-field foul pole.

The image of Fisk, using body English to "wave" the ball fair, became as iconic a shot as any associated with the game. In terms of both TV coverage—the isolated shot of Fisk became the TV industry gold standard for reaction shots—and postseason baseball drama, the 1975 loss, painful though it was, was truly a Fall Classic.

But as if to ratchet up the anticipation, the Sox kept finding ways to torment their loyalists. With each visit to the World Series, they would inch closer, only to suffer the most excruciating of defeats.

The 1978 season saw the Red Sox cough up a 14-game lead, fall out of first, and then, just as incredibly, win their last eight games to force a one-game playoff with the New York Yankees for the division.

Redemption, right?

Wrong.

On an otherwise glorious New England autumn day, the Red Sox lost to the Yanks 5–4 as light-hitting shortstop Bucky Dent's three-run homer in the seventh inning helped erase a 2–0 lead.

That game would mark Yastrzemski's last shot at a championship and further subjugate the Sox to their longtime rivals. Losing was bad enough. Losing to the Yankees—and Bucky f'n Dent—made it officially unbearable.

Each time, fans would allow themselves to believe that this surely would be the year. And each time, cruelly, the Red Sox would find ways to dash those hopes.

In that sense, 1986 was the mother of all disappointments.

After a miraculous comeback against the California Angels in the American League Championship Series, there seemed reason to believe that, for the Red Sox, This Year—the tempting reward implicitly promised in the team's "Wait 'til Next Year" quest—was finally here. And when the Red Sox took a 5–3 lead over the Mets in the 10th inning of Game 6 and were one strike away from winning their first title since 1918, the stage was quite literally set.

The visitors' clubhouse in New York's Shea Stadium had been outfitted for a celebration for the ages. The champagne was on ice, the trophy awaited a presentation, and Jean Yawkey, widow of owner Thomas A. Yawkey, was escorted into the room to bear witness to what her husband had missed. Even the scoreboard at Shea flashed congratulations to "the 1986 World Championship Boston Red Sox."

Then, the Sox found a way to elevate losing to performance art.

After a series of two-out hits, an errant pitch, and, most notorious of all, a ball that squirted through first baseman Bill Buckner's legs, the Red Sox squandered a two-run lead and lost in the most unpredictable fashion imaginable.

The Red Sox came to be known as a cursed franchise. No matter the circumstances, they would inevitably lose in the end. Naturally, this sense of fatalism became a heavy burden.

"I don't know nothin' about history," fumed 1986 manager John McNamara, when reminded of Boston's bleak past, "and I don't want to hear about choking or any of that crap."

▲ Bill Buckner walks off the field dejected after his error in Game 6 of the 1986 World Series.

And still, the Sox weren't done. In 2003, the team carried a late-inning lead into Game 7 of the ALCS at Yankee Stadium. But starting pitcher Pedro Martinez, tiring and the life on his fastball fading, was inexplicably left on the mound as the Yankees mounted an eighth-inning comeback.

In the 11th, the dream died. The Yankees' Aaron Boone swatted a knuckleball from Tim Wakefield into the left field seats. Just like that, Red Sox history featured a new candidate for worst defeat ever.

The decision to leave Martinez in the game—against all reasonable suggestions to the contrary—cost manager Grady Little his job. The loss itself nearly cost Red Sox fans their central nervous systems.

But the Promised Land was, this time, just around the corner.

The Curse Ends

The 2003 season had been such a soul-crushing near-miss that something had to be done to improve the roster and address the deficiencies. In young general manager Theo Epstein, the Red Sox had the right man for the job.

A New England native, the Yale-educated Epstein had experienced the abject heartache of the 1986 World Series loss to the Mets, like millions of other fans raised on a cocktail of hope and despair. Unlike the others, however, Epstein was in position to do something about it.

For starters, he replaced manager Grady Little with Terry Francona, though at the time, Francona hardly seemed like a dugout elixir. Over four years with the Phillies in his only other managerial stint, he had experienced four losing seasons.

But Epstein put Francona through a series of interviews and game simulations to guard against the sort of brain freeze Little had experienced with his season on the line. From that process, Epstein had a sense that Francona, a baseball lifer whose father had played in the big leagues, possessed the intangibles to win in a market like Boston.

Francona could be self-deprecating, innovative, and a good communicator, all of which served him well as he took on what some would label a thankless task: changing the doomed history of a franchise in a city battered by past disappointment.

Next, Epstein addressed the pitching staff. In the span of a few weeks, he swung a trade for Curt Schilling, who had a well-earned reputation as a pitcher who thrived on the biggest of stages. He also signed free-agent closer Keith Foulke to fortify a bullpen that Little couldn't trust when it mattered most.

The Red Sox qualified for the playoffs as the wild-card entry and made quick work of the Anaheim Angels, setting up—wouldn't you know it?—a return engagement with the hated Yankees in the ALCS.

To say it didn't begin well would be a massive understatement. Boston lost the first two games in New York as Schilling's injured ankle withered and the Red Sox appeared badly outclassed. A 19–8 pasting by the Yankees back at Fenway in Game 3 was humbling and seemed to set the stage for a sweep by Boston's tormenters.

Trailing in Game 4 of the ALCS, Red Sox owners began drafting their own version of a concession speech, congratulating their rivals for vanquishing them in such a convincing manner. It was a humiliating if gracious act.

The players, though, had other ideas. Before the game, despite having just lost a home playoff game by 11 runs, the team was surprisingly loose, a reflection of their fun-loving nature and perhaps Francona's ability to set a relaxed tone.

On the field and in the clubhouse, Kevin Millar, a journeyman bat ticketed for sale to Japan before Epstein intervened and claimed him off waivers, warned of the consequences the Yankees would face if the Sox, trailing 3–0 in the series, managed to win even a single game.

THE FIVE GREATEST GAMES IN
RED SOX HISTORY

5. Taking It to the Twins in Game No. 162 (October 1, 1967)

A bunt from Jim Lonborg to start a comeback. A huge hit from Carl Yastrzemski to key the big inning. And, as the final out settled into Rico Petrocelli's glove, setting the stage for the Red Sox's first AL pennant in more than two decades, it was, as broadcaster Ned Martin described it, "pandemonium on the field."

4. Henderson the Hero—Game 5, 1986 ALCS (October 12, 1986)

Ultimately, this postseason, like so many others in club history, ended badly. But this one, facing elimination against the California Angels, had all the markings of a great game—lead changes, extra innings, and Dave Henderson as the Hero du Jour thanks to his game-changing home run in the ninth and game-winning RBI in the 11th.

3. It's Over—Game 4, 2004 World Series (October 27, 2004)

There wasn't anything particularly memorable about this game—no late-inning rally or true drama. But hey, when you haven't won it all in 86 years, how can you leave this one off? Years—decades!—from now, Red Sox fans will be able to tell you where they were when Keith Foulke fielded the comebacker and threw to Doug Mientkiewicz at first for the final out against the Cardinals.

2. Staying Alive—Game 4, 2004 ALCS (October 17, 2004)

This is where The Comeback began. On the verge of being swept by the Yankees, the Sox were down to their final three outs when they tied the game in the ninth inning. Then they won it in the 12th on a David Ortiz walk-off homer. It would take three more wins to complete the journey, but the seed was first planted in this game.

1. Fisk's Wave—Game 6, 1975 World Series (October 21, 1975)

True, this World Series against the Reds would end in disappointment, but there's no denying the drama associated with this Fall Classic classic. This one had it all—great momentum swings, pinch-hit homers, and, of course, Carlton Fisk's game-winner in the 12th off the left-field foul pole. Not just the greatest game in Red Sox history, this is on a short list of the greatest games ever. Pete Rose sensed it at the time. "This is some kind of game, isn't it?" he asked Fisk as he stepped to the plate to lead off the 11th. It sure was.

SAFE! Dave Roberts steals second in Game 4 to keep the ALCS hopes alive.

"Don't let us win tonight," shouted Millar to no one and everyone, as casually as he might be before a spring training game.

Millar already had the future mapped out in his head.

"They've got to win tonight," he theorized, "because if we win, we've got Pedro (Martinez) coming back (in Game 5) and then Schilling will pitch Game 6, and then you can take that fraud stuff and put it to bed. Don't let the Sox win this game."

Still, the Sox trailed in the ninth inning against Yankees closer Mariano Rivera. A less enviable situation could not be imagined. But then Millar walked, and Dave Roberts, pinch-running, stole second. A single by Bill Mueller then scored Roberts and forced extra innings.

CURSE CLOSED Closer Keith Foulke lifts catcher Jason Varitek after recording the last out in Game 4 of the 2004 World Series.

In the 12th inning, David Ortiz hit a walk-off homer, and the Red Sox lived another day. That day, too, was won by Ortiz, with a walk-off single in the 14th.

The series then shifted to New York for Game 6, with the Red Sox feeling emboldened by their two home wins. Schilling, who had suffered a torn tendon in his ankle earlier in the postseason and pitched poorly in Game 1, returned freshly sutured, after an emergency procedure that featured a tendon from a cadaver. With blood staining his sock, Schilling heroically won Game 6, forcing a winner-take-all Game 7.

In any other season, there would have been the feeling that the Red Sox would find a way to lose the ultimate showdown. It was, after all, seemingly part of their DNA. But this time, all the pressure bore down on the Yankees. How had they allowed the Red Sox off the mat? Were they really about to become the first baseball team to lose a best-of-seven series after winning the first three games?

As a matter of fact, they were. The Red Sox romped to a 10–3 victory and celebrated with family and friends on the field at Yankee Stadium, where, almost exactly a year earlier, they had suffered the most soul-squashing defeat.

One hurdle remained. But the Sox had come too far to stop now, and they rolled over the Cardinals—oh, the irony—in four games.

In a remarkable show of sportsmanship and Midwestern hospitality, Cardinals management decided to open the gates in the late innings to allow any Sox fans, many of whom had made the trip from New England, to watch history up close.

In a jubilant visitors' clubhouse, Schilling toasted "the greatest Red Sox team ever," and Epstein sagely noted that 1918—the mere mention of which had become a taunt by New York fans and others—"is now just another year in which the Red Sox won the World Series."

In the days and weeks that followed, New Englanders continued to celebrate the win. Grave sites were festooned with Red Sox championship pennants, a tribute to those who hadn't lived long enough to see the day. Had it been worth the wait? For those fortunate to see it, the answer was, in the moment at least, an unequivocal "yes."

Rivals: The Yankees

During long stretches of their shared histories, it sometimes seemed as if the Yankees and Red Sox weren't even playing the same game.

And truth be told, they weren't.

While the Red Sox were often finishing at the bottom of the standings, the Yankees were evolving into baseball's winningest franchise. From 1936 through 1964, a period of 29 seasons, the Yankees won 22 pennants and 16 World Series. During that time, the Red Sox won exactly one pennant. That's it.

During this era, the teams' superstar outfielders, Boston's Ted Williams and New York's Joe DiMaggio, were often compared. And on one liquor-soaked evening, the icons were nearly traded for one another by their imbibing owners. But in the end their résumés were strikingly different: DiMaggio played in 10 World Series, while Williams reached only one.

That type of disparity made it hard to consider the Red Sox and Yankees true rivals. The Yankees had other things and teams about which to worry. The Red Sox may have been the Yankees' closest AL rivals geographically for much of their history, but in actuality, the two teams were a million miles apart.

Then, the Red Sox entered an era in which they were actually competitive on a semi-regular basis, and the relationship changed. The teams famously brawled on the field in

1967, evidence of Boston's newfound confidence. Until then, the Red Sox hardly seemed worth thinking about.

In the early 1970s, there were ugly home-plate collisions, beanball wars, and bench-clearing brawls. Hard-nosed competitors like Lou Piniella and Carlton Fisk tangled at home plate. During one brawl, Red Sox lefty Bill Lee wrestled with Graig Nettles and Mickey Rivera—at the same time—and came out of the exchange with a wrenched shoulder and renewed hatred of what he labeled "Steinbrenner's brown shirts."

Things came to a head in 1978. As the Red Sox raced out to a huge lead in the AL East, the Yankees appeared on the verge of imploding. In June, Reggie Jackson and manager Billy Martin came to blows in the visitors' dugout at Fenway. The combination of the Red Sox romping and the Yankees flailing at one another proved to be the perfect storm for Red Sox fans, who were unsure of what development pleased them more.

Alas, the euphoria didn't last. The Yankees completed an early September sweep—known as "the Boston Massacre"—and overtook the Red Sox in the standings. Only a furious late charge by the Red Sox, which required them to win their final eight games, forged a tie for first in the East and a one-game playoff.

The '78 playoff game was one for the ages, full of star power—including five future Hall of Famers: Boston's Carl Yastrzemski, Jim Rice, and Fisk, and New York's Jackson and Goose Gossage—and plot twists. A three-run homer by light-hitting shortstop Bucky Dent proved to be the game's biggest hit. The final at-bat featured Gossage getting Yaz to pop up with the potential tying run on third base.

The two teams then had a sort of baseball détente until the late 1990s when, because of an expanded playoff format, it was possible for the first time for them to meet in the postseason. And they did meet in October on three separate occasions between 1999 and 2004. In 1999, the Yankees, in the middle of another dynastic run that would see them win four World Series in the span of five seasons, simply outclassed the Red Sox in five games.

They met again in 2003. That series saw Yankees bench coach Don Zimmer, who had been the Red Sox manager in 1978, charge Pedro Martinez during an on-field brawl.

THE FIVE GREATEST TRADES IN
RED SOX HISTORY

The most famous transaction in the Red Sox's formative years saw them sell off a young pitcher (and occasional outfielder) to the rival Yankees. Name of Ruth—perhaps you've heard of him? But not every move Boston made was as ill advised.

5. $150,000 to the Philadelphia Athletics for Jimmie Foxx (December 10, 1935)

This was mostly a cash deal (three lesser players also changed hands), but a smart one for the Sox, who landed one of the game's greatest sluggers. Foxx played for seven seasons in Boston and hit .320 with a .605 slugging percentage. In 1938, the first baseman also became the first player in Sox history to hit 50 home runs, a team record until David Ortiz arrived.

4. Casey Fossum, Brandon Lyon, and two minor leaguers to Arizona for Curt Schilling (November 28, 2003)

After falling short in the 2003 postseason, the Red Sox needed another big-game pitcher to pair with Pedro Martinez. They got their man in Schilling. Two World Series titles—in 2004 and 2007—followed.

Ultimately, the Red Sox took the Yanks to Game 7 and held the lead late into the game. But then Martinez, Boston's ace, faltered, manager Grady Little froze, and the rest is history. In the 11th inning, the inevitable took place: Aaron Boone homered, the Yankees moved on, and the Red Sox went home to lick familiar but festering wounds.

When the Red Sox and Yankees weren't battling on the field, they were competing for players. In 2003, the Yankees outmaneuvered Boston for Cuban export Jose Contreras,

3. Nomar Garciaparra (multi-team deal) for Orlando Cabrera and Doug Mientkiewicz (July 31, 2004)

Garciaparra was unhappy with a contract extension offer and had become injury-plagued. Red Sox general manager Theo Epstein rolled the dice in a big way at the deadline and landed a replacement shortstop in Cabrera and a defensive upgrade at first base in Mientkiewicz, both of whom were instrumental in the World Series win three months later.

2. Heathcliff Slocumb to Seattle for Derek Lowe and Jason Varitek (July 31, 1997)

This was an absolute steal: Slocumb had flamed out as Red Sox closer, so the Sox sent him to the Mariners and obtained Varitek—who would enjoy a 15-year career with Boston and serve as its captain—and Lowe, who would win 20 games one season, save 40 games another, throw a no-hitter, and win three games in the 2004 postseason.

1. Carl Pavano and Tony Armas Jr. to Montreal for Pedro Martinez (November 18, 1997)

Pavano and Armas were two highly regarded young pitchers, but Martinez only became one of the two or three greatest pitchers in franchise history. Pavano would go on to a 14-year career in the big leagues, winning 108 games, but that was a slight achievement when matched against Martinez's Hall of Fame numbers.

leading then–Red Sox president Larry Lucchino to utter, "The Evil Empire extends its tentacles into Latin America."

Finally, in December 2003 the Red Sox thought they had obtained MVP shortstop Alex Rodriguez from the Texas Rangers, only to have the deal scrapped when the Major League Baseball Players Association disallowed some of the contractual concessions Rodriguez had made to help facilitate the deal.

Months later, after Boone—irony, again—blew out his knee playing basketball, the Yankees entered the picture, landed Rodriguez to be his replacement, and persuaded the superstar to switch to third base. Even off the playing field, the Red Sox couldn't win.

All of that, however, was merely a warm-up for 2004. In a midseason showdown, Bronson Arroyo drilled Rodriguez with an inside fastball. Rodriguez, taking his time to complain on his way to first, soon found catcher Jason Varitek's mitt in his face, and the benches cleared. The photo of Varitek's face-washing became iconic throughout Boston, but full revenge came that October.

Once again, Rodriguez found himself in the center of another on-field confrontation in the ALCS showdown, earning further ridicule by attempting to slap the ball out of Arroyo's glove in Game 6. Ultimately the joke was on him, as the Red Sox became the first baseball team to overcome a 3-to-0 deficit in a seven-game series.

How sweet was that comeback? Sweet enough that when the Sox went on 10 days later to capture their first championship in nine decades, more than a few Red Sox fans considered that to be the season's second-most noteworthy achievement.

OH SO GOOD The Red Sox await David Ortiz after his 12th-inning home run in Game 4 of the 2004 ALCS.

BOSTON RED SOX
MOUNT RUSHMORE

Pedro Martinez (1998–2004)

Martinez spent seven seasons with the Red Sox and in that span established himself as one of the game's most dominant and charismatic aces. At a time when PED-bloated sluggers were cranking homers at a record pace, Martinez was posting ridiculous numbers. He owns the best winning percentage (.760) in team history and also has the best strikeout-per-nine-inning ratio and lowest opponent batting average.

Four times an All-Star with the Red Sox, Martinez also won two Cy Young Awards in Boston and should have won an MVP, but some writers left him off their ballots in 1999 because he was a pitcher. In 2000, Martinez won his second Cy Young in a row with an earned-run average nearly two runs lower than the next-closest qualifying pitcher.

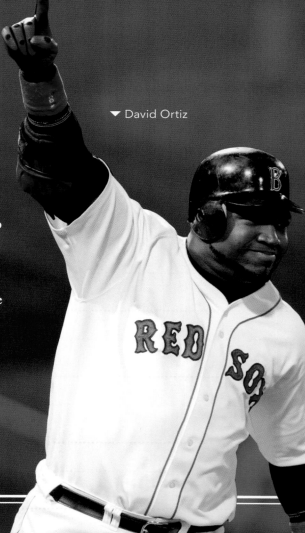

▼ David Ortiz

Martinez may have been slight of frame, but his larger-than-life persona made his Fenway starts events and attracted a new generation of Latino fans to the ballpark.

David Ortiz (2003–2016)

Signed as a free agent after being non-tendered by the Minnesota Twins, Ortiz turned out to be the biggest bargain in franchise history. He began as a platoon option at designated hitter but soon emerged as the team's key run producer and slugger.

Ortiz, who played key roles on World Series–winning teams in 2004, 2007, and 2013, earned a reputation as a winner. He almost single-handedly brought the Sox back from the dead in the 2004

ALCS against the Yankees with game-winning, extra-inning hits in Games 4 and 5. Indeed, he became recognized as one of baseball's top clutch performers, with his October exploits and propensity for walk-off heroics.

Moreover, like his Dominican countryman Pedro Martinez, Ortiz was among the most engaging and personable of Red Sox stars, loved by fans and opponents alike. Big Papi became the face of Boston after the marathon bombings in 2013 with an unforgettable (if slightly profane) speech vowing the city would survive the tragedy.

Carl Yastrzemski (1961–1983)

Yaz was in the unenviable position of replacing Ted Williams in left field, and those inevitable comparisons haunted him for a long time. He won a batting title in his third season, but he didn't come into his own until his Triple Crown season in 1967.

That year stands as one of the greatest in modern baseball history, as Yastrzemski led the league in batting average, homers, and RBIs while winning a Gold Glove in left field. Every time the Sox needed a big hit that season, it seemed that Yastrzemski provided it.

His onetime teammate Ken "Hawk" Harrelson called it the best single season he has ever seen anyone have, and he's not alone. Yastrzemski went on to win another batting title and became the first American Leaguer to hit 400 homers and collect 3,000 hits. His farewell season of 1983—his 23rd, all with the Red Sox—concluded with a memorable and fitting farewell to the fans at Fenway Park.

Ted Williams (1939–1960)*

Perhaps more than any other sport, baseball has always engendered the best debates: Who's the fastest player? Who's the strongest? Who's the best this or the best that? But for decades, there's been little argument to this question: Who's the greatest hitter of all time? The answer would seem fairly obvious, even to the casual fan.

That would be the guy who compiled a lifetime on-base percentage of .482, the guy who reached base almost 4,700 times in his career, the guy who belted 521 homers despite missing nearly five full seasons due to military service, the guy who was the last player to hit .400 in a single season, the guy who hit .316 or better in 18 of his 19 seasons in the big leagues.

He may have been an indifferent fielder and a disinterested base runner. He never won a World Series and won just one pennant in a career that spanned four decades. But there's little doubt as to who baseball's greatest hitter ever is: that would be Ted Williams.

*Did not play in 1943–1945 due to military service

BOSTON RED SOX
BEST OF THE REST

Wade Boggs (1982–1992)

Boggs was an eight-time All-Star with the Red Sox and won an unprecedented five batting titles, second only to Ted Williams's six in team history. He posted seven 200-hit seasons and played more games at third base than anyone who ever wore the uniform. How good was he offensively? Only Ted Williams had a higher career batting average for the Sox.

Roger Clemens (1984–1996)

Clemens had a rocky career in Boston and left town in an ugly fashion. But there's no denying how great he was while with the Red Sox, starting with a season for the ages in 1986 when he was the AL MVP and Cy Young Award winner. He won three Cy Young Awards and was robbed of another in 1990. He racked up strikeouts and innings pitched and was among the most charitable and philanthropic players in modern Sox history.

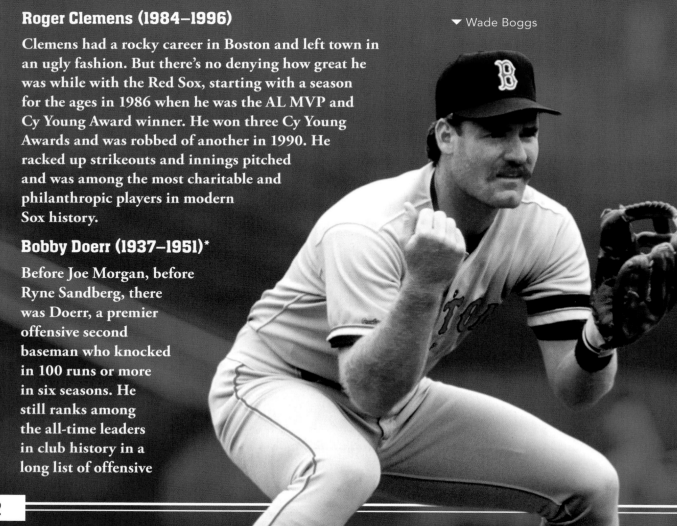

▼ Wade Boggs

Bobby Doerr (1937–1951)*

Before Joe Morgan, before Ryne Sandberg, there was Doerr, a premier offensive second baseman who knocked in 100 runs or more in six seasons. He still ranks among the all-time leaders in club history in a long list of offensive categories: hits, runs, doubles, walks, total bases, and extra-base hits. He also held his own on defense, setting a major league record for second basemen in 1948 by fielding 414 consecutive chances without an error. A member of the Baseball Hall of Fame, Doerr was one of the most popular players of his era, especially in Boston, and for good reason.

Did not play in 1945 due to military service

Manny Ramirez (2001–2008)

He was eccentric enough that his behavior eventually was shrugged off with a popular three-word phrase: Manny being Manny. But in the batter's box, he was unparalleled in his achievements and ranks among the greatest right-handed hitters of the modern era. He hit for average and for power and was the MVP of the history-making 2004 World Series team. Like others, his stay in Boston ended in controversy, but his impact on the team is undeniable.

Jim Rice (1974–1989)

Rice was one of the premier sluggers in the 1970s and 1980s with a remarkably consistent output. In his MVP season of 1978, he became the first AL player since Joe DiMaggio to amass 400 total bases or more in a season. In his final year of eligibility, he was elected to the Baseball Hall of Fame in 2009 after a career in which he batted .298 with 382 homers and 1,451 runs batted in.

Tris Speaker (1907–1915)

A member of two World Series–winning teams, he still ranks second in franchise history in triples and steals and third in batting average—more than a century after he was traded in a salary dispute. Speaker was also a superb outfielder. His nine splendid seasons in Boston helped make him part of baseball's second class of elected Hall of Famers.

Cy Young (1901–1908)

Young spent more time in Cleveland than in Boston, but he was with the Red Sox long enough to win 192 games, a record that stood until Clemens tied it decades later. In an admittedly different era, he won 20 games or more six times and twice won more than 30 in a season. When the award for pitching excellence is named after you, you've had a pretty good career, and about 40 percent of that career was spent in Boston.

CHAPTER 5
THE COLLEGES

I t's one of Boston's great ironies that, despite being home to more than 30 colleges and universities totaling more than 150,000 students, the city has long been known for its devotion to professional, rather than collegiate, sports.

Television ratings for college football and basketball pale in comparison with other regions of the country. In the entire state of Massachusetts, there are but two Football Bowl Subdivision (or FBS) programs—Boston College and UMass, with the latter having transitioned to Division I only in 2013. And although some alums faithfully follow their schools, it usually takes a unique player or series of events to capture the attention of the average local sports fan.

But big followings or not, there's plenty to invest in when it comes to the Boston college sports scene, beginning with tradition.

◀ Though no longer competing for national championships, Harvard's football team is hard to match in terms of a tradition.

Harvard, unsurprisingly, has among the richest of sports traditions, with a football program that dates to 1873. Owing largely to this longevity, Harvard is among the 10 winningest football programs in NCAA history, and Crimson football has won seven national championships, although the most recent was in 1919.

The championship drought is evidence of how the sport has changed in the past century and, from a competitive standpoint, passed by programs such as Harvard's. Still, within its own sphere, Harvard has more than acquitted itself as a perennial contender in the Ivy League. And from the standpoint of tradition—without regard to attendance or impact nationally—there's little that can beat Harvard vs. Yale. Known simply as "The Game," the series began in 1873 and stands as the third-oldest rivalry in college football. While it's true that the Crimson vs. the Elis hardly matters when it comes to determining the national championship or major bowl berths, many of college football's modern traditions—from the use of mascots and fight songs to the implementation of rules and protocol—date back to Harvard–Yale.

If the program itself isn't historic enough, there's always Harvard Stadium, housed across the Charles River from the main Cambridge campus in the Allston section of Boston. It has been in use since 1903, making it the second-oldest athletic facility still in use in the country and one of just four to be designated as a National Historic Landmark.

The atmosphere at the stadium, as might befit such a venerable setting, is unique. The crowds at Harvard games will never be confused with those attending, say, Oklahoma–Texas. Instead, on a beautiful fall day, the stadium and its environs more closely resemble a cocktail party, with fans dressed in blazers and other upscale finery.

HAIL FLUTIE Quarterback Doug Flutie celebrates during the Cotton Bowl win against Houston on January 1, 1985.

If Harvard represents Boston's past, then the football program at Boston College is the city's most accomplished in the modern era. After years as an independent, BC became a charter member of the Big East. Now the school competes in the Atlantic Coast Conference, matched with traditional football powers such as Clemson and Florida State.

BC's transition to the ACC has had its ups and downs, with some winless in-conference seasons. But the program's glory days aren't all in the distant past, such as on New Year's Day 1941 when, under legendary coach Frank Leahy, BC beat Tennessee in the Sugar Bowl to lay claim to a share of the national championship.

More recently, the Eagles enjoyed some of their greatest success in the 1980s, led by quarterback Doug Flutie. A scrambling, diminutive passer, Flutie enjoyed a tremendous career at the Heights, as the campus is known. In his most famous moment, Flutie in 1984 led BC to a last-minute comeback win over Miami in what some describe as the greatest college football game ever played. He also directed the Eagles to a Cotton Bowl win over Houston to close out his senior season.

Football is king among college sports, but it's far from the only sport for which Boston-area schools are known. All four of the region's Division I men's college basketball programs have made appearances in the NCAA Tournament, with BC reaching the Elite Eight in 1982 and 1994. After an absence that spanned 66 years, Harvard made four straight visits to the tourney from 2012 through 2015. Northeastern ended a 21-year streak of its own with a March Madness appearance in 2015, while BU has made it at least once a decade since the 1980s. Harvard has also claimed national titles in women's rowing and lacrosse, plus several more in other sports from before the NCAA era, while at various times the schools have found success in sports like field hockey, soccer, and track and field. But there's little question as to the sport at which the four schools have thrived the most: hockey.

Boston College and Boston University have each won five men's national titles, with Harvard adding its own in 1989. Women's programs have been successful, too, with Harvard, BU, and BC each having claimed runner-up finishes. And a 2017 study confirmed that all four schools have produced US Olympians in the sport, with BC (32), Harvard (29), and BU (28) trailing only the University of Minnesota (68).

So say what you will about Boston being a pro sports town. As the die-hard fans know, the city's college programs can more than hold their own.

THE TOP FIVE COLLEGE SPORTS MOMENTS
IN BOSTON HISTORY

5. Holy Cross vs. Oklahoma, men's basketball (March 25, 1947)

Holy Cross isn't in Boston, of course. But Worcester isn't far away, and to be fair, Holy Cross, then without a gym on campus, played its home men's basketball games at Boston Garden. The Crusaders, featuring freshman guard Bob Cousy, beat Oklahoma 58–47 in the NCAA title game to become the first Massachusetts-based school to win a national basketball title.

4. Boston University vs. Miami (Ohio), men's hockey (April 11, 2009)

BU scored twice in the final 59.5 seconds to force overtime in the 2009 NCAA men's hockey championship game. In OT, defenseman Colby Cohen scored at 11:47 for a 4–3 victory to capture BU's fifth national title.

3. Boston College vs. Notre Dame, football (November 20, 1993)

This series has taken on the moniker of "the Holy War," as Boston College and Notre Dame are the only two Catholic institutions competing at the Football Bowl Subdivision level. They've played 24 times over the years, but this, the fifth meeting between the teams, was the first BC victory. Notre Dame was ranked No. 1 in the country and BC No. 17, but BC, after a furious fourth-quarter Irish comeback, pulled out a 41–39 win on David Gordon's 41-yard field goal with no time remaining.

2. Harvard "Beats" Yale, football (November 23, 1968)

Yale owned a 16-game winning streak, but both teams came into the game unbeaten and untied for the first time since 1909. Behind backup quarterback Frank Champi, the Crimson rallied to score 16 points in the final 42 seconds. Thanks to the comeback, the 29–29 tie felt like a win for Harvard, thus the famous newspaper headline and subsequent documentary.

1. Doug Flutie's Hail Mary, football (November 23, 1984)

Boston College, ranked 10th in the nation, was an underdog at 12th-ranked Miami on the day after Thanksgiving in 1984. In the closing minutes, BC trailed 45–41 as quarterback Doug Flutie took his team from his own 20-yard line to the Miami 48 with 28 seconds remaining. Dropping back to his own 37-yard line, Flutie somehow heaved the ball nearly 65 yards in the air. Gerard Phelan slipped past the Hurricanes secondary to catch the ball in the end zone in what has been called by some the greatest college football game ever.

The Beanpot

Few college sporting events have more tradition or history than the Beanpot, held annually in February. On the first Monday night, two men's games are played, with the championship game—and consolation game—played the following Monday. The women play on the Tuesdays of the same two weeks.

The fact that the tourney attracts little attention outside of New England makes it a Boston-centric sporting event, through and through. To those outside the area, it means virtually nothing; to those with a rooting interest, it can mean almost everything.

The event dates to 1952, when it was designed as a midwinter showcase for the area's four Division I college hockey programs: Boston College, Boston University, Harvard, and Northeastern.

Held in its first year at the historic Boston Arena and then for four decades at Boston Garden, the Beanpot has called TD Garden home since 1996. Over the years the tournament has evolved into one of the highlights of the Boston sports calendar, and since 1979, the event also has included a women's tournament as well, though that's played at campus rinks. Yet for all its significance and tradition, the Beanpot's initial goal was far more modest.

"It was designed as filler," said Jack Grinold, the longtime sports information director at Northeastern and unofficial historian of the tournament. "I mean, it was originally the

BOSTON'S BEST Future NHL star Jack Eichel of Boston University skates around a Harvard player en route to the 2015 Beanpot title.

first two nights after Christmas in 1952. It was to help the (Boston) Arena on off nights. It's way, way beyond that now."

Indeed, the Beanpot is a coming together of four schools, like a tribal ritual. It attracts students, alums, those without an obvious tie to any of the participants, and, not incidentally, NHL and national team scouts who look past the pageantry and history in search of potential players.

The fact that it's played on successive Monday (or Tuesday) nights allows the Beanpot to grab the interest and attention of local fans. After all, what else is so compelling on a winter weeknight? By the time the Beanpot gets under way, the Super Bowl has often been played, the NHL and NBA schedules have entered the midseason doldrums, and the promise of baseball—and warmer weather—is still weeks away.

In that way, the Beanpot offers a winter respite, a chance to revel in a sport that has a relatively narrow following and celebrates the rivalries and history.

What makes the Beanpot, an annual sellout at the Garden, such a unique event is the proximity of the schools involved. There are other college hockey tournaments in the country—the Great Lakes Invitational stands as one obvious example—but although that event draws from various points across Michigan, the Beanpot features schools that are, in some cases, only blocks from one another.

On a cold winter night, you could take the "T"—Boston's MBTA subway and trolley car mass transit system—from one campus to the next in less time than it takes to play a period of hockey.

"It's not just that the same schools are there," said Harvard hockey coaching legend Bill Cleary, "but that they are so close to each other."

One year, famously, the school's supporters were a little too close to one another. As New England got buried by a blizzard in February 1978 and a storm dumped almost three feet of snow in the Boston area, the tournament went on as scheduled. While the two games were being played, snow built up outside the old Boston Garden, making passage anywhere impossible. Undaunted, the fans remained inside content to watch the games. When the games finished, thousands of fans had no choice but to spend the night inside the venerable barn.

For much of its existence, the men's Beanpot has been dominated by two participants: Boston College and Boston University. Rare is the year that at least one of the two schools doesn't take part in the title game.

Need proof? Until Harvard won the title in 2017, a college hockey fan would have to go all the way back to 1993 to find a year in which either BU or BC didn't win the Beanpot. Together, the two powerhouses, located on opposite ends of Commonwealth Avenue, have won more than two-thirds of the titles. But Harvard and Northeastern alumni tell themselves

▲ *From left*, Harvard's Jamie Hagerman, Alison Kuusisto, and Vanessa Bazzocchi celebrate with the women's Beanpot trophy after beating Boston College in 2002.

that this year—or maybe next—will be the year in which their alma mater's luck changes. Northeastern, at least, has had more luck on the women's side, with 16 wins to Harvard's 14 through 2017.

The tournament has been home to Hobey Baker and Patty Kazmaier award-winners—given annually to the nation's top collegiate players—and countless future NHL stars and Olympians. But mostly, it has been stubbornly, defiantly, proudly, part of the Boston sports landscape, a tournament like no other.

BOSTON'S TOP FIVE
COLLEGE ATHLETES

Harry Agganis, Boston University (1948–1950, 1951–1952)

Agganis was a three-sport star at Boston University, and what a star. In football, he was BU's first first-team All-America selection, setting school records for touchdowns and passing yards. He also played basketball and baseball. He was chosen by the legendary Paul Brown as a potential replacement for quarterback Otto Graham but decided to play baseball for the hometown Red Sox after owner Tom Yawkey outbid Brown by $10,000. Tragically, he died of a pulmonary embolism at the age of 26.

Bill Cleary, Harvard (1953–1955)

Even before he helped Team USA win the Olympic gold medal in 1960 and became the legendary hockey coach at his alma mater, Cleary was a standout player for the Crimson. He still holds seven school scoring records and was a first-team All-American in 1954–55, when he led the Crimson to a Beanpot title—scoring five goals in the title game—and a spot in the Frozen Four. Cleary also lettered in baseball at Harvard.

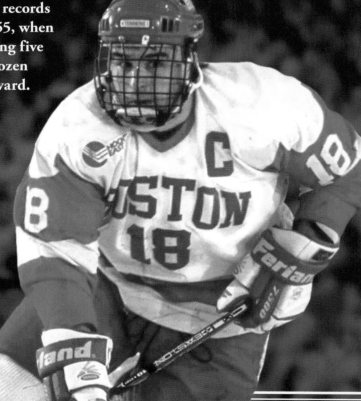

▼ Chris Drury

Chris Drury, Boston University (1994–1998)

Even before he arrived at BU, Drury had been accustomed to winning, leading his Trumbull, Connecticut, team to the 1989 Little League World Series title. As a freshman hockey star, he helped lead the Terriers to an NCAA title. He was chosen as the Hockey East Defensive Player of the Year three times and earned the Hobey Baker Award as the nation's top player. He went on to a long, successful NHL career.

Doug Flutie, Boston College (1981–1985)

An undersized quarterback with quick feet and a howitzer for an arm, Flutie brought the Heights to great heights in the early 1980s, quarterbacking Boston College to several top-10 rankings in national polls, a trip to one of the most prestigious New Year's Day bowls (beating Houston in the Cotton Bowl), and, of course, the last-minute comeback against Miami, a game that ranks among the most exciting ever played. Flutie put BC on the college football map and captured the Heisman Trophy as the nation's most outstanding college football player. He also made BC a destination school nationally and helped ramp up the football team's recruiting for years to come.

Reggie Lewis, Northeastern (1983–1987)

Lewis, who played basketball at famed Dunbar High School in Baltimore, scored 2,708 career points at Northeastern, still a school record. The Huskies won the ECAC North all four years of Lewis's collegiate career, and more impressively, qualified for the NCAA Tournament each time, something Northeastern hadn't done before or since. His retired number hangs in the rafters. He was a first-round draft pick by the Celtics, but died tragically at 27 after a cardiac event during an offseason practice. The Reggie Lewis Track and Athletic Center in the Roxbury section of Boston stands today as a lasting tribute to his legacy as an athlete and philanthropist.

▶ Reggie Lewis

CHAPTER 6
BOSTON AND THE OLYMPICS

When it's not being referred to as the "Hub of the Universe," Boston is sometimes called the "Athens of America," a nod to the city's association with education and culture. Perhaps it's only fitting then that Boston enjoys deep Olympic roots, dating to the first modern Olympics in 1896 in Athens, Greece.

James Connolly, a proud son of South Boston, requested a deferment from his studies at Harvard to compete in Athens. The school said no, but he went anyway and became the first modern Olympic champion with his victory in the triple jump. The win earned Connolly a silver medal—then the highest honor—and he later placed second in the high jump and third in the long jump. When he returned to the Boston area a local hero, Harvard reconsidered and invited him back, an offer he pointedly declined. Nonetheless, Boston established a link to the Olympics, one that lasts until this day.

◀ South Boston's James Connolly dropped out of Harvard and won the first event in the first modern Olympic Games in 1896.

Over the years a sizable chunk of US Olympic men's and women's hockey teams have consisted of Boston-area natives and others born elsewhere who attended one of the area's four Division I hockey programs.

This includes the 1980 "Miracle on Ice" team. It's impossible to have the most memorable moment in US Olympic history—indeed, one of the most memorable in all of sports history—without the contributions of Mike Eruzione, a Winthrop native and Boston University standout, or Jim Craig, who grew up in Easton and also attended BU. Fittingly, women who hailed from those same schools helped make up the backbone of the US women's hockey teams that have thrived since the sport's 1998 Olympic debut.

Of course, hockey is just one of many Olympic sports that featured Boston-area contributors. From figure skaters Nancy Kerrigan and Paul Wylie to gymnasts Aly Raisman and Alicia Sacramone, the modern Olympics always seem to have a little Boston flavor.

Even the local pros have had their Olympic moments. Back in 1956, when competition was limited to amateurs, the great Bill Russell won a gold medal just before turning pro and beginning his legendary NBA career. As Olympic sports began allowing participation by professional athletes, the connection to Boston has only grown stronger with athletes like Larry Bird. The Celtics legend was part of the 1992 Dream Team that captured the gold.

After contributing so many athletes to Team USA over the years, Boston for a time was intent on inviting the Games to town. In January 2015, the US Olympic Committee announced with great fanfare that Boston was its choice to bid for the rights to host the 2024 Olympics. However, public opinion, which initially backed the effort, quickly turned.

Opposition centered on concerns about cost overruns and the impact the Games would have on traffic in an already notoriously congested city. The detractors spoke of higher taxes and the potential impact the bid would have on the city's infrastructure. Ultimately, they succeeded. The bid lasted just seven months. By July 2015, the USOC had pulled the plug on Boston.

Instead, the USOC got behind Los Angeles as its host representative, and the International Olympic Committee indeed selected that city to host the Games—but in 2028, rather than 2024.

To some, the failed bid represented the parochial nature of Boston. To others, it was symbolic of the region's sometimes Byzantine political process, with too many

▲ Though best remembered for the dramatic 1994 Olympics, Stoneham native Nancy Kerrigan competed also in the 1992 Olympics, medaling in both.

seeking credit and too few willing to take responsibility. And to others still, the rejection was seen as an example of a city willing to take a fiscally responsible stand rather than fall prey to a shiny—and overpriced—international bauble. Whatever the reason, it became obvious: For Bostonians, the Olympics would continue to be a spectator sport from afar.

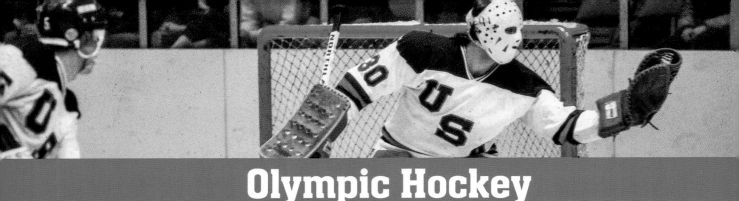

Olympic Hockey

Boston is home to an Original Six franchise in the NHL, four Division I college hockey programs, the Beanpot tournament, and countless public rinks where the game is learned and loved. So it's only logical that the city's greatest connection to the Olympics would be the sport of hockey.

In the 20th century, Boston-area skaters played huge roles in three incredible Olympic hockey tournaments, resulting in gold medals each time.

Two decades before "The Miracle on Ice," the biggest achievement in US hockey was a feat now known as "The Forgotten Miracle." With the 1960 Winter Games being held in Squaw Valley, California, the home team was mostly an afterthought. Most observers favored heavyweights like Canada and the Soviet Union, giving Team USA little chance to even reach the medal round. Instead, the scrappy American team, led by Cambridge brothers Bill and Bob Cleary, wrote a different story.

Team USA surprised everyone with early-round wins over Australia, Czechoslovakia, Sweden, and Germany. Having advanced to the medal round, the Americans kept on winning. They dispatched Canada 2–1, and then they came from behind to beat the Soviets 3–2 before walloping Czechoslovakia 9–4 to win the gold medal. Bill Cleary scored the go-ahead goal, which was fitting because he was the tournament's leading scorer with 12 points. Bob Cleary added eight points.

During his Harvard career, Bill had offers to turn pro from both the hometown Bruins and the Montreal Canadiens. Instead, he maintained his amateur status so he could compete at the 1956 and 1960 Games.

"I'm glad I did," said Cleary, who would go on to serve as Harvard's longtime men's hockey coach. "I would have missed two Olympics."

The US Olympic program had to be glad Cleary did, too. In his time, there was a geopolitical backdrop as the 1960 Games, in particular, were being played against the undertones of an escalating Cold War. That Cold War backdrop was still omnipresent 20 years later in 1980. Later that summer, with the Soviets hosting the Summer Games in Moscow, the United States would boycott in protest of the Soviet Union's invasion of Afghanistan. But in February, in tranquil Lake Placid, New York, the Winter Games went on as planned.

Eighteen years before NHL players would be allowed in the Olympics, the US team was filled with amateurs. The American roster, coached by Herb Brooks, was mostly made up of kids from the upper Midwest—with a heavy emphasis on Minnesota—and New England. Four of the 20 players were natives of the greater Boston area: defenseman Jack O'Callahan from Charlestown, forward Dave Silk from Scituate, goaltender Jim Craig from Easton, and forward Mike Eruzione from Winthrop. All four played their college hockey at Boston University.

Local ties notwithstanding, Team USA was considered a massive underdog, seemingly no match for the fully loaded Soviets, nor for that matter any number of European teams or their neighbors to the north, Canada, which had skipped the previous two Olympics.

Instead, Team USA surprised many with a first-round tie with Sweden, followed by wins over Czechoslovakia, Norway, Romania, and West Germany. That set up a critical medal-round matchup against the Soviets.

Winners of the previous four Olympic gold medals, and five of the last six, the Soviet team had little reason to worry about the Americans. Only weeks earlier in an exhibition game at Madison Square Garden, the same Soviet squad had flattened the Americans 10–3. Then in its first five games of the Olympic tourney, the mighty Soviet machine had outscored opponents 51–11. And in goal, the Soviets had the world's best goaltender in Vladislav Tretiak. Now, in the medal round, what chance did the plucky Americans have?

Plenty, as it turned out. The teams played even at 3–3 for the first 50 minutes before Eruzione took a feed from linemate Mark Pavelich. From the top of the faceoff circle, Eruzione got off a quick wrister that beat Vladimir Myshkin, who, to the surprise of just about everyone, had replaced Tretiak in net after the first period.

The Americans clung to the one-goal lead as though their lives depended on it and, as the final seconds counted down, play-by-play announcer Al Michaels provided one of the most iconic calls in sports broadcasting: "Do you believe in miracles? Yes!"

In the immediate aftermath of the victory, Craig skated from his crease and wrapped himself in the US flag. He could be seen searching the stands of the Olympic Fieldhouse, mouthing: "Where's my dad? Where's my dad?"

As much as any other moment, that image—the handsome goalie, draped in his country's flag, searching for his father—is the one that lingers from that moment, decades later.

MIRACLE ON ICE Captain Mike Eruzione and Team USA stand atop the medal podium as 1980 Olympic champions.

It's often forgotten that the highly dramatic win over the Soviets did not, in fact, clinch the gold medal for Team USA. For that, the Americans needed to beat Finland two days later, which they did. Nonetheless, it was the win over the Soviets that resonated with the American psyche, and it was from that game that Eruzione became a national hero.

Americans who had never before watched a hockey game regarded him with wonder. He traveled, appeared on the talk-show circuit, became a popular pitchman, and became synonymous with American pride. He was also one of just seven members of the US team never to play in the NHL. At 25, he was considered too old, and his skills likely wouldn't have transferred to the faster, rougher NHL game.

But Eruzione harbored no regrets.

"It's not like there were big offers," he said years later, "and I just thought it was time to move on and do something else."

Hadn't he already done enough?

Although Boston's influence on the US men's Olympic team has ebbed and flowed over the years—there were no Massachusetts natives on the 2014 US men's team—the city has had another opportunity to contribute since 1998, when women's hockey became an Olympic sport.

A relatively new sport, women's hockey had held its first world championship just eight years earlier in 1990 and, going into the 1998 Games in Nagano, Japan, Canada had won each of the four world titles to date. But the Americans had finished second each time, and with five Massachusetts natives on the roster and a Massachusetts native as coach, they made history in Nagano, stunning Canada 7–4 in the preliminary round and then beating

LEGACY Team USA's Alex Carpenter, of North Reading, scores against Canada in the 2014 Olympic gold-medal game.

the Canadians again 3–1 in the gold-medal game. Forward Sandra Whyte, a former Harvard player from Saugus, assisted on the second goal and then potted the empty netter to seal it.

That would long be the high point for the US women, but players born or schooled in the Boston area continued to play outsized roles on Team USA, which won a bronze and three silver medals in the next four Olympics. In the early years it was Harvard standouts such as Angela Ruggiero and Julie Chu who led Team USA, while in 2014 it was Boston College forward Alex Carpenter—daughter of former Massachusetts schoolboy star Bobby Carpenter, the first American-born player selected in the first round of an NHL draft— who stepped up. Her team-leading four goals helped clinch another silver medal in Sochi, Russia. That 2014 team, by the way, was coached by Harvard's Katey Stone.

BOSTON'S TOP
OLYMPIANS

Bill Cleary (1956, 1960)

In 1960, he was Mike Eruzione before Eruzione shocked the world two decades later. Cleary, too, was a Boston-area native who attended a local school (Harvard, in this case) and was the hero of the underdog US men's hockey team that upended the Soviets in Squaw Valley, California. Four years earlier he helped the Americans win a silver medal at the 1956 Games in Cortina d'Ampezzo, Italy.

James Connolly (1896, 1900)

Boston prides itself on its place in history—sports and otherwise—so it's entirely fitting that this son of Boston was the first modern Olympic champion. Connolly, a 27-year-old Harvard undergrad, left school to compete at the first modern Olympic Games in 1896 in Athens, Greece, where he won the triple jump, then known as "hop, skip, jump," to become the first Olympic champion in more than 1,500 years. Connolly also finished second in the high jump and third in the long jump. Four years later at the 1900 Olympics, Connolly finished second in the triple jump, and four years after that he covered the 1904 Olympics in St. Louis as a journalist for the *Globe*.

Jim Craig (1980)

Craig will forever be remembered for his stellar play in the 1980 Olympics at Lake Placid, when, as the goaltender for the US men's hockey team, he was spectacular in making 36 saves in Team USA's upset of the Soviets.

Kayla Harrison (2012, 2016)

Raised in Ohio but trained in Wakefield, Harrison captured gold medals in judo in both the 2012 and 2016 Games. Her 2012 win marked the first time an American won a gold medal in the sport, and it came after she escaped a sexually abusive coach and began working with Wakefield's esteemed coach Jimmy Pedro.

Mike Eruzione (1980)

A few years removed from playing at Boston University, Eruzione was painting houses in the summer before going off to play on the 1980 US men's hockey team, which he captained. Eruzione wasn't the fastest or most skilled skater or toughest player on the squad, but coach Herb Brooks saw in the Winthrop native a tireless work ethic with sound instincts, and he loved his natural leadership ability. That belief paid off when Eruzione scored the winner against the Soviets, sending a bunch of college kids to victory over the most fearsome hockey team in the world. Do you believe in miracles? You bet.

Nancy Kerrigan (1992, 1994)

Kerrigan had already won a bronze medal at the 1992 Games in Albertville, France, and was considered a favorite to win the gold in 1994 in Lillehammer, Norway. But at the US Figure Skating Championships in January, a month before the Games, Kerrigan was attacked by someone hired by rival Tonya Harding. Kerrigan, from Stoneham, recovered and went on to win silver in the 1994 Games, but for a long time, she was unfortunately thrust into the middle of the sporting world's biggest scandal.

▶ Mike Eruzione

Karen O'Connor (1988, 1996, 2000, 2008, 2012)

Competing in women's equestrian events, O'Connor, from Bolton, took part in an astonishing five Olympiads from 1988 through 2012, winning a team silver medal in Atlanta in 1996 and a team bronze in Sydney, Australia, in 2000. At the 2012 Games in London, England, she was the oldest competitor at 54.

Aly Raisman (2012, 2016)

Known for her powerful tumbling and steely consistency, Raisman's floor routine clinched the Olympic gold medal for the US women's gymnastics team at the 2012 Games in London, one of two gold medals—and three overall—that she won that year. If that wasn't enough, the team captain led the Americans to gold again in 2016 in Rio de Janeiro, Brazil. Overshadowed by once-in-a-generation teammate Simone Biles, Raisman, of Needham, quietly put together a truly dominant performance in Rio, which also included silver medals in the all-around and floor exercise. After those Games, she used her platform to speak out against systematic sexual abuse within US gymnastics.

Alicia Sacramone (2008)

A Winchester native, Sacramone is the second-most-decorated US gymnast in world championships history, with a total of 10 medals. In her only Olympic appearance, in 2008 in Beijing, China, Sacramone helped the American team win a silver medal. However, her team finals performance was marred by falls on floor exercise and balance beam.

John Thomas (1960, 1964)

Thomas was the first high jumper to clear more than seven feet while competing collegiately. On the Olympic stage, the Boston native jumped spectacularly but was always edged by Soviet rival Valery Brumel. Thomas finished second to Brumel in 1964 in Tokyo, Japan, and was third to the Soviet Union's Robert Shavlakadze and Brumel in 1960 in Rome, Italy.

Jenny Thompson (1992, 1996, 2000, 2004)

Thompson was born in Danvers—though she later moved to Dover, New Hampshire—and was one of the most dominant swimmers in modern history, winning 12 Olympic medals in the butterfly and freestyle, including eight relay gold medals, from 1992 through 2004.

◀ Aly Raisman

CHAPTER 7
SOCCER IN NEW ENGLAND

One by one, they arrived. In another time—heck, even a month earlier—it would have been almost impossible to even imagine, but here they were. On June 27, 1999, a crowd of 50,484 people showed up at Foxboro Stadium to watch the US women's national soccer team take on North Korea. It was the final game of Pool A at the 1999 FIFA Women's World Cup, and the middle of a summer in which Mia Hamm and Co. captured the country's attention en route to a world title.

The game was in some respects a formality. The US team, having already clinched a spot in the quarterfinals, rested some starters. And after a crowded North Korea defense stymied any scoring chances in the first half, the Americans broke out for three unanswered goals in the second. Goalie Briana Scurry, a Minnesota native who played collegiately at UMass, earned the shutout, her second in three games.

◀ Shannon MacMillan of the United States evades a North Korea defender during their 1999 FIFA Women's World Cup match at Foxboro Stadium.

SUPERSTARS Portuguese star Eusébio, *left*, was briefly the main attraction for the Boston Minutemen while Brazilian Pelé, *right*, led the New York Cosmos.

The 1999 World Cup was a wake-up call telling the world that people really do care about women's sports. And for the Boston area, this game—and the four others played at Foxboro Stadium—proved to be the next big step in the sport's long journey to relevance in the New England sports scene.

Dating to the 1920s, a series of men's pro soccer clubs attempted to make inroads throughout New England, but none lasted long. The best bet came in the 1960s and 1970s. Three separate teams made a go of it in the original North American Soccer League, that which also famously featured Pelé and the New York Cosmos. Alas, none lasted in the boom-or-bust NASL.

The Boston Beacons folded after just one season in 1968, the Boston Minutemen folded after a three-year run from 1974 to 1976, and the New England Tea Men (named in tribute both to the Boston Tea Party and to the team owners, the Lipton tea company) stayed for only three years before moving to Jacksonville, Florida, after the 1980 season.

Still, the sport's appeal continued to grow nationally and regionally, and the Boston-area immigrant base—with fans of Irish, Italian, and Portuguese descent—helped develop the sport at the grassroots level in New England.

Then the 1990s changed everything, in both Boston and the rest of the United States. The World Cup had existed since 1930, largely without the United States. Both sides had an interest in changing that, and in 1988 FIFA awarded the 1994 World Cup to the United States. With it came promises of a long-elusive men's professional league. Organizers for both the tournament and the nascent pro league, sensing Foxboro's potential—with easy access from Providence, Rhode Island, and the New Bedford–Fall River, Massachusetts, area, which had a host of ethnic groups attracted to the game—bet on New England.

The 1994 World Cup brought with it unprecedented crowds, even so far as the World Cup was concerned. Foxboro was no exception, as upwards of 50,000 people showed up to see such exotic matches as Bolivia vs. South Korea and Nigeria vs. Greece. Six games were played at Foxboro, including a memorable quarterfinal in which ponytailed Italian star Roberto Baggio slyly rounded Spain's goalie to notch the winning goal in the 88th minute.

The foundation set, New England next turned its attention to the professional game. Future Patriots owner Robert Kraft, who already owned Foxboro Stadium, was awarded one of 10 charter franchises of Major League Soccer, set to begin play in 1996. The future was bright for soccer in New England, and the new team, the Revolution, would at times show flickers of living up to the sport's potential.

Unfortunately for those hardcore fans—the supporters groups like the Midnight Riders, the Rebellion, and La Barra, who've stuck by the Revs—that peak potential still lives somewhere in the future. At a time when MLS success is often coupled with an urban, soccer-centric stadium and an engaged, generous ownership, the Revs are still playing in cavernous Gillette Stadium, far from the center of Boston, and amidst regular groans about neglect from the team's owners.

Despite that, for a period the Revolution were the league's version of the Buffalo Bills— meaning they were pretty damn good, besides that whole "never winning a championship" thing. With the imposing Shalrie Joseph holding down the defensive midfield, creative midfielder Steve Ralston slipping passes just where they needed to be, and premier MLS sniper Taylor Twellman scoring the goals, New England reached the MLS Cup four times in six seasons, from 2002 to 2007. The two times they fell short of the title game, the Revs lost in the conference finals. If it was any consolation, at least, the Revs at least came away with the US Open Cup title, the American version of England's FA Cup, in 2007.

All the while, soccer has continued to grow in and around Boston. Foxborough has made itself a regular home of the US national teams—including, infamously, a pre-viral viral moment in 1997 when goalie Kasey Keller tried to clear a ball in the first minute of a game, only to have it bounce off the forehead of a nearby Mexican player and roll into the net for a goal. Nonetheless, the national teams keep coming back, and so do the international teams. In 2016, Gillette Stadium was home again to top-tier games during the Copa America Centenario, a tournament featuring the national teams of North and South

America. European professional teams continue to return for preseason exhibitions just about every summer, too.

Not to be lost in the sport's progression is the women's game. The Boston Breakers debuted in 2001 in the Women's United Soccer Association, a professional league meant to capture the momentum of the 1999 World Cup. After that league folded in 2003, the Breakers returned in the new Women's Professional Soccer in 2009. The team survived the downfall of that league, too, and moved on in 2013 to the National Women's Soccer League, which appears to have finally stabilized the women's pro game. Alas, the league's stability couldn't save the Breakers, who were unable to find new ownership and folded ahead of the 2018 season.

▲ Grenada-born midfielder Shalrie Joseph controls the ball during the 2006 MLS Cup against the Houston Dynamo.

Still, the Breakers had their highlights and occasional big names, such as Connecticut natives Kristine Lilly and coach Tony DiCicco. Lilly was a legend for the US national team, while DiCicco guided the team to historic Olympic and World Cup titles. And even with the team's demise, the NWSL's managing director remained hopeful that the Breakers would soon be back to capture that ever-present potential: "It's a market that we believe in," she said.

THE TOP FIVE SOCCER STARS IN
BOSTON HISTORY

The modern era of soccer is still growing, but the Boston area has produced and nurtured its share of stars in the sport.

5. Billy Gonsalves (1927–1929)

In an era almost unrecognizable to today, Gonsalves was one of the first US soccer stars. Though born in Bristol, Rhode Island, the midfielder found pro success with the Boston Wonder Workers of the American Soccer League before playing in the first two World Cups, in 1930 and 1934. Though in a different era, the Americans' semifinal appearance in 1930 remains their best finish.

4. Steve Ralston (2002–2009)

Although Ralston racked up more than 30 caps with the US national team, he made his living as one of MLS's best and most reliable passers. He ended his career with the most assists in Revs (73) and MLS (135) history.

3. Shalrie Joseph (2003–2012)

At 6'3", Joseph was at the heart of the Revs' run of runner-up finishes. Born in Grenada, Joseph became a New England fan favorite through his strong play in the defensive midfield. Revs fans to this day will argue that the team's all-time leader in games and minutes played was, for a time, one of the best to ever suit up in the fledgling league.

2. Kristie Mewis (2009–2012 at BC, 2014–2016 with the Breakers)

A native of Hanson, which is just south of the Boston metro, Mewis was a four-year star at Boston College, where she was named to the All-Atlantic Coast Conference team in her sophomore, junior, and senior years, while becoming a semifinalist for the Hermann Trophy, given annually to the nation's top male and female college soccer players. She is BC's all-time women's leading scorer and has played pro soccer for a number of years, including a stint for the Breakers.

1. Taylor Twellman (2002–2010)

Some players just click in MLS, and Twellman was one of them. After joining the Revs from a German team in 2002, the St. Louis native scored at a rate unmatched in MLS play before concussions prematurely ended his career in 2010. Although he got in 30 games with the US national team, Twellman was the quintessential MLS star—dominant in the league but never quite the same anywhere else. And it will never be known how he would have fared in Europe, as the Revs turned down any offer to buy his services. They had good reason: Twellman was a goal-scoring machine in MLS, knocking in 23 as a rookie and 16 in 2007, while in 2005 he scored 17 goals en route to an MLS MVP award. Now a popular broadcaster, Twellman remains the franchise's all-time leader in goals scored.

"In all my time in the MLS," Revs coach Steve Nicol said, "he has been the purest and best goal scorer in the league, without a doubt."

▶ Taylor Twellman

137

CHAPTER 8

THE ONES THAT GOT AWAY

Boston's main pro sports franchises have enough history, tradition, and championships that they stand on their own. But when it comes to the history of pro sports in Boston, they're not alone. Not by a long shot. There have been a host of other teams that share a place in Boston sports history.

Although unfathomable today, Boston was once a two-team baseball town. In fact, the city's National League entry predated the Red Sox by three decades. That team—which was known by a slew of nicknames before officially adopting the Braves moniker in 1912—began play in 1871 at South End Grounds and joined the NL in 1876.

There were some good times. In 1914, the Braves rebounded from last place in midsummer to complete a stunning sweep of the Philadelphia Athletics in the World Series. The next year, they moved to Braves Field, mere

◀ Members of Boston's National League team, then known as the Beaneaters, pose together with the New York Giants on the first day of the 1886 baseball season.

▲ Tackle Albert Glen "Turk" Edwards played for Boston's NFL team from 1932 until it moved to Washington in 1937.

miles from Fenway Park. At the time, Braves Field had the largest seating capacity in the NL at 40,000. However, the magic from South End Grounds was lost.

The team struggled for the next 20 years, a period that included a string of 10 losing seasons, before a mid-1940s boost. Backed by the starting pitching duo of Warren Spahn and Johnny Sain, the Braves won 91 games to capture the 1948 NL pennant. However, they lost to the Cleveland Indians in the World Series. Across town, meanwhile, the Red Sox had built a following during their successful early-1900s period, and the presence of Ted Williams helped them hold onto it during the leaner years. The Braves had no such luck with attracting fans, and after the 1952 season they moved to Milwaukee.

In football, the Boston Redskins, known for one season as the Boston Braves, played five seasons in Boston as part of the original NFL. The team began play at Braves Field in 1932 before moving to Fenway Park in 1933 and changing its nickname to Redskins.

The Redskins were largely a mediocre lot during their stay in Boston, but a late-season surge in 1936 sent them to the NFL Championship Game. However, owner George

Marshall was so disappointed with home crowds of fewer than 5,000 fans that he forfeited home field for the title game and moved it to the Polo Grounds in New York. The Redskins lost that matchup to the Green Bay Packers and the next year moved to Washington, DC.

A decade later, the NFL tried again with a Boston-based franchise called the Yanks, but the team suffered through five losing seasons and poor attendance. The Yanks were dissolved after the 1948 season and their rights transferred to New York. Boston was without pro football until the formation of the American Football League's Patriots in 1960.

Hockey had its also-rans, too. The success of the Bruins and the growth of pro hockey stemming from a big NHL expansion effort in 1967 whetted the appetite for more hockey. The result was the upstart World Hockey Association, which arrived on the scene in 1972 and placed one of its charter franchises, the New England Whalers, in Boston. The team split its home schedule between the ancient Garden and the even-more-ancient Boston Arena, but despite capturing the first Avco Cup as WHA champs, the Whalers never gained a steady fan following. After a second season in Boston, the team moved to Hartford in 1974, where it remained—with some games played in Springfield, Massachusetts—after being folded into the NHL in 1979.

Boston has had its share of more obscure teams, too. Capitalizing on the tennis boom of the 1970s, World Team Tennis arrived in 1974 with a charter franchise known as the Lobsters. After one unsuccessful season on the court and at the box office, the franchise was contracted. But just in time for the next season, the Philadelphia Freedoms were bought and relocated to Boston, where they, too, were renamed the Lobsters. Among the early investors in the franchise was Robert Kraft, who would buy the Patriots two decades later.

▲ Martina Navratilova, *right*, joined Massachusetts Governor Michael Dukakis during a Boston Lobsters event in 1977.

The Lobsters, playing matches in Boston and elsewhere in New England, lasted four more seasons, the last two of which would introduce the tennis world to a young Martina Navratilova, who was named the league's female MVP in 1978. The Lobsters had the best record in the league, but it didn't help with fan support, and months after the 1978 season, the franchise folded. (Another iteration of the Lobsters returned for a decade, beginning in 2005.)

Since the Patriots arrived in 1960, Boston's four major teams have managed to stick around. But the world of sports is full of peripatetic teams, coming and going, often the result of expanding leagues or new ventures. Boston had its share of those, too. Some left a bigger mark on the city than others. Gone, but maybe not totally forgotten, are such teams as the Boston Demons (Australian rules football), the Boston Whitecaps (men's ultimate), and the three local NASL entrants. Meanwhile, the tradition rolls on for the Boston Cannons (men's lacrosse), the Boston Pride (women's hockey), and the Boston Derby Dames (roller derby).

For now.

FOUR ATHLETES
BOSTON MISSED OUT ON

Boston has had its share of great athletes to cheer on over the years, but had it not been for franchise relocations these four might have joined in on the tradition.

Henry Aaron

The man many still regard as baseball's all-time home run king was in the Braves' minor league system while the team was in Boston. He didn't make his major league debut until 1954, the Braves' second season in Milwaukee. How might baseball history have changed had his feats come while playing in Boston? How would Aaron's presence have changed the city's troubled racial history? Sadly, we'll never know.

Sammy Baugh

Another bit of bad timing. The very next season after the Boston Redskins shifted to the nation's capital, Baugh made his debut for the team and went on to a long, illustrious career in which he was recognized as one of the greatest quarterbacks in NFL history.

Mark Howe

Three years after the New England Whalers exited Boston for Hartford, the team signed defenseman Mark Howe as a free agent. Howe, of course, was the son of all-time great Gordie Howe. But Mark himself was a Hall of Fame defenseman who played 22 seasons in the WHA and NHL.

Eddie Mathews

Mathews was a rookie in 1952, the final season for the Boston Braves, and he enjoyed a fine season, good enough to finish third in the NL Rookie of the Year voting. He went on to hit 512 homers, knock in 1,453 RBIs, and gain entrance into Cooperstown. But 16 of his 17 seasons were played after the Braves left Boston—first for Milwaukee and later Atlanta.

CHAPTER 9

ONLY IN BOSTON

Some events on the Boston sports calendar truly are one of a kind. Take the Beanpot, for example, Boston's tribal college hockey tournament, which takes place the first two Monday nights each February. This is truly a local event, one that is everything to its core audience but registers little interest outside the city limits.

Then there's the Boston Marathon, the world's oldest annual marathon, which can be traced back to 1897, a year after the very first marathon was held at the first modern Olympics. Once the purview of local runners—the first race had just 15 entrants—the Boston Marathon long ago morphed into a truly international competition, drawing competitors from every continent. Every year amateurs and professional runners alike flock to the city for the third Monday in April, a day celebrated as Patriots' Day, a uniquely Boston holiday.

◀ A fan and a runner high-five before the 2014 Boston Marathon begins in Hopkinton.

For many competitive runners, merely getting the chance to run Boston is a lifelong achievement. Since the early 1970s, Boston has been the rare marathon that requires most entrants to meet a qualifying standard for each age-group, and those standards continue to get more difficult. This has helped the marathon become the gold standard in the running world. *Are you running Boston this year?* No further clarification is needed.

> "To us in New England, we just say bowling. Bowling is candlepin. That's regular bowling for us. We would say 'Big Ball Bowling' if we were talking about the other kind."
>
> - Liz *MOORE*
> EXECUTIVE DIRECTOR OF THE INTERNATIONAL CANDLEPIN BOWLING ASSOCIATION.

In the rowing community, the same can be said for the Head of the Charles Regatta, every bit the staple of the fall sports season as the Marathon is for the spring. On the second-to-last full weekend of October, the Charles River, which separates Boston and Cambridge, is home to this prestigious competition, attracting competitors from all over the world, with spectators making the pilgrimage from far and wide.

Boston, it must be said, enjoys some sports endemic to the city and region. Take candlepin bowling, a variation on the more widely accepted ten-pin game that features much smaller balls and consists of three balls per round instead of the more common two.

There's also the practice of traditional high school football rivals facing off on Thanksgiving morning. Let Texas have Friday Night Lights; in the Boston area, it's Thursday Morning games, an athletic table-setter on Turkey Day.

The Marathon

Every spring since 1897, the Boston Marathon has served as a harbinger of the new season: If the runners are running from suburban Hopkinton to the finish line on Boylston Street, the promise of warmer weather can't be far behind.

After starting in the western suburbs, the marathon course makes its way through seven communities as runners navigate winding roads and challenging changes in terrain. "Heartbreak Hill," near the Boston College campus, is the most demanding section of the course and frequently separates the best from the rest of the field.

For nearly its first 80 years, the race was strictly amateur. Winners received a laurel wreath made of olive branches, a nod to the race's Olympic roots. By the 1980s, as road races became more lucrative for elite marathoners, the Boston Athletic Association, the race's governing body, reluctantly began offering prize money provided by corporate sponsorship. In that respect and in others, the race's evolution has mirrored societal changes. Not until 1972 did the Boston Marathon officially allow female contestants, and this change was somewhat forced upon it.

In 1967, Kathrine Switzer somewhat surreptitiously entered the race as "K.V. Switzer," while not disclosing her gender. She was issued an official race number only to be attacked on the course by race director Jock Semple, who attempted to tear away her number and get her disqualified. Switzer nevertheless persisted and finished the race. Five years later women were officially included in the field, and 50 years after her historic debut, Switzer returned to the course and raced again, this time celebrated as a pioneer.

The race hasn't been without other controversies. In 1980, Rosie Ruiz traveled much of the course by subway and emerged from a crowd about a mile from the finish line. Once her ruse was discovered, she was disqualified.

The race has experienced tragedy, too. In 2013, with the winners having already completed the race on a shining spring day, two bombs detonated in a terrorist act near the finish line. Four people were killed and hundreds wounded. The bombing sent the city into a panic, with a weeklong manhunt for the perpetrators resulting in a shelter-in-place order for nearby Watertown. One suspect was captured, found guilty, and sentenced to the death penalty. Another was killed in a police pursuit.

The shocking attack galvanized the city and the region, and "Boston Strong" became a motto and a symbol for the city's resilient recovery. For decades, the Red Sox have hosted a Patriots' Day game with an 11 a.m. start time, specifically designed to allow fans to watch the game and then pour into nearby Kenmore Square to witness the marathoners. In 2013, five days after the tragedy, that relationship grew. In pregame ceremonies at Fenway, slugger David Ortiz insisted in a famously emotional speech that Boston was, in fact, "our fucking city," and no one would curtail the citizens' freedom. When the Sox captured the World Series title that fall, their celebratory duck boat parade made a special stop at the marathon's finish line to honor the memory of the victims.

And who can forget April 21, 2014? With emotions still raw, the first Boston Marathon after the bombing began as usual in Hopkinton. A little more than two hours later, the

WINNER Four-time US Olympian Meb Keflezighi crosses the finish line first at the 2014 Boston Marathon.

Eritrea-born, San Diego–bred Meb Keflezighi arrived on Boylston Street by himself. Racing toward Copley Square, the 39-year-old was greeted by cheers from a defiant crowd that was twice as large as usual. Crossing the finish line at 2 hours, 8 minutes, 37 seconds, Keflezighi wrapped himself in an American flag. One year after the race's lowest moment, and at an age when he should have had no businesses contending, he was the first American since 1985—and first US man since 1983—to win the Boston Marathon.

As that moment exemplified, the Marathon is typically a joyous event. Along the route, an estimated half-million spectators provide emotional support, cups of refreshing water, and sometimes offers of kisses from college students.

Each year the marathon is an excuse to day drink for some and to welcome spring's arrival for others, and a recognition of the stamina, dedication, and commitment of athletes the world over. But mostly, it's a celebration of the traditions, the history, and the unique nature of an athletic competition that truly is one of a kind.

The Regatta

Though perhaps dwarfed by the Boston Marathon in terms of participation and international attention, the Head of the Charles Regatta, held each October, has its own place on Boston's calendar.

Set on the Charles River, which bisects Boston and Cambridge, the course could be something out of a picturesque New England tableau. As the autumn foliage begins to unveil itself, spectators line both sides of the river and take in a competition that began in 1965 and was originally introduced to break up some of the monotony for local college rowing teams training for intercollegiate schedules.

The winding course includes six bridges, and collisions—particularly near the race's conclusion—are not uncommon. Teams begin the race in 15-second intervals, but the course can become congested.

More than 60 events are held over the weekend—the regatta expanded to two days in the late 1990s—and 10,000 rowers in nearly 2,000 boats participate. Local and faraway college teams compete, as do rowing clubs. Competitors, grouped by age, include divisions for high school students all the way up to the grand-veteran class for those who are 80-plus.

Spectators watching from folding chairs or blankets give the event a festive backdrop. Some root for entrants from their alma maters—the course passes both the Harvard and

RACE DAY Crowds watch the rowers in the 2017 Head of the Charles Regatta.

Boston University campuses along with nearby Northeastern's boathouse—and others are content to observe the competition amid the typically mild fall weather.

The event serves as a celebration of so much of what makes Boston special: the city's waterways, its skyline, its institutions of higher learning, and its devotion to athletic competition, pure and traditional.

"I think most folks around here would compare Head of the Charles to Christmas, because it's just a huge family reunion. People I've rowed with in high school, college, the national team are all here for this one weekend."

- Andrew *CAMPBELL JR.*
HARVARD GRAD AND 2016 US OLYMPIAN IN
LIGHTWEIGHT DOUBLE SCULLS

If the Marathon introduces spring and the promise of warmer weather, the Head of the Charles serves as a goodbye to summer, staged in autumnal beauty, a farewell to one sports year, begun on the streets six months earlier and ended on the water.

It's the outdoor Boston sports calendar year bookended by marvelously, distinctively Boston events.

10 BOSTON ATHLETES
WE CAN'T FORGET

Kelly Amonte Hiller

Amonte Hiller grew up in Hingham and starred in lacrosse at Thayer Academy (as her brother Tony, a former NHL star, did in hockey). She went on to win two national championships at the University of Maryland and has since won a stunning seven national championships as the women's lacrosse coach at Northwestern. When her Wildcats won their first national title in 2005, they became the first Midwestern team to do so in the sport.

Pat Bradley

Bradley is one of the greatest to play on the LPGA Tour, where she competed for 21 years. During that time the Westford native won 31 tour events, including six majors. In 1986, she came within one major of recording a grand slam. Bradley is a member of the World Golf Hall of Fame and is the aunt of PGA pro Keegan Bradley.

Tony Conigliaro

Conigliaro was the very embodiment of "Local Boy Makes Good." Born in Revere, just north of Boston, and raised in Swampscott, Conigliaro signed with the hometown Red Sox and reached the major leagues at age 19, hitting 24 homers as a rookie in 1964. A year later he became the youngest home run champion in baseball history, clubbing an American League best 32. He also became the youngest American League player to reach 100 career homers.

In 1967, he was struck in the eye by a pitch by the California Angels' Jack Hamilton, a beaning that nearly killed the Red Sox outfielder. Miraculously, Conigliaro returned to baseball in 1969 and, though the vision in his left eye was permanently damaged, hit 56 homers over the next two seasons. He attempted a second comeback in 1975. Tragically, he was felled by a stroke in 1982 and died in 1990 at age 45.

Patrick Ewing

Born in Jamaica, Ewing moved to Cambridge at age 11 and attended Cambridge Rindge and Latin. At Georgetown he became one of the dominant basketball players in the history of the Big East Conference, reaching the national championship game three times, and was named consensus first-team All-American three times. He enjoyed a long, successful professional career, mostly with the New York Knicks, with whom he was an 11-time All-Star.

Marvin Hagler

Though he was born in Newark, New Jersey, Hagler adopted Brockton as his hometown. With a career record of 62–3–2 and 52 knockouts, Hagler was one of the most dominant fighters of his era and is generally regarded as among the best middleweights ever. He engaged in unforgettable battles in the ring with some of the biggest names in the sport in the 1980s, defeating Roberto Duran and Thomas Hearns before losing a controversial split decision to Sugar Ray Leonard.

Rocky Marciano

A native of Brockton, Marciano is considered one of the greatest heavyweights of all time, posting a 49–0 record with 43 knockouts. He won the heavyweight title in 1952, and then defended it successfully six times before retiring at 32. Though he never lost a fight, some boxing historians have argued that Marciano failed to face another truly great heavyweight in his prime. Both

Jersey Joe Walcott and Archie Moore were 38 when they fought—and lost to—Marciano. But Marciano can hardly be blamed for the quality of his opponents.

At 5'10" and 185 pounds, his hard-charging style in the ring made him a fan favorite and helped, at least partly, inspire the fictional character of Rocky Balboa in the series of films starring Sylvester Stallone. He also earned praise for his ability to take a punch (he was knocked down just twice as a pro). Marciano further cemented his legacy by refusing numerous lucrative offers to come out of retirement, not wishing to blemish his perfect record or his place in heavyweight history.

Marciano died tragically young, the night before his 46th birthday, when the private plane he was flying in crashed in a storm.

Chris McCarron

Boston native McCarron is viewed as one of the greatest horse racing jockeys ever, having earned $264 million in winnings, with 7,141 wins, including six in Triple Crown races. He's a member of the US Racing Hall of Fame.

Francis Ouimet

Arguably the greatest American amateur golfer ever, Ouimet grew up across the street from the fabled The Country Club in his native Brookline. Born to modest means, he caddied at the club, where he learned the game. He won the US Open in 1913 and the US Amateur in 1914 and 1931.

Jeremy Roenick

Born in Boston, Roenick was one of the best American-born players in NHL history. Over 18 seasons, he scored 513 goals and had 703 assists. Only three US-born players have recorded more points in the NHL.

Keith Tkachuk

A Melrose native, the left wing is one of five US-born players with 500 goals or more in the NHL and one of nine with at least 1,000 career points. He came to embody the phrase "power forward" while playing for Winnipeg, Phoenix, St. Louis, and Atlanta.

◀ Rocky Marciano

BOSTON'S MOUNT RUSHMORE

This book is full of legendary athletes who have made Boston their professional home over the decades. Many are, quite rightly, considered among the best ever to play their respective sports, and many have been honored with enshrinement in various halls of fame.

Still, there's a difference between all-stars—and even all-time greats— and a handful of Boston athletes who belong in another sports stratosphere. These stars have done more than break records and win championships; they've transcended their sports, become household names, and are singularly identified with their teams. These four Boston athletes established legacies that likely will never be topped, and above all others deserve a spot on Boston's Mount Rushmore.

◀ Few cities can claim four athletes as dominant as Boston's big four.

Tom *BRADY*

QUARTERBACK - NEW ENGLAND PATRIOTS (2000—)

The most amazing thing, really, about the long list of Tom Brady's accomplishments—the five Super Bowl wins, the multiple MVPs, the countless late-game comebacks, the undefeated regular season—is the sheer improbability of it all. Because, when you look at it with some detachment and logic, Brady shouldn't have had the magnificent career he has had.

He was a sixth-round draft pick in 1999. Sixth! Those sorts of players come and go all the time, interchangeable pieces with little promise of success. Some get a little playing time, some get consigned to practice squads, but most get spit out altogether by the wood chipper that is the NFL.

But what others never accounted for—and perhaps what only Brady himself understood—is the enormous drive, ambition, and sheer will that has driven him from the beginning. Never mind what others thought of him, or how he was regarded. He wasn't so much trying to prove the doubters wrong—though some of that might have fueled him. Brady had his own goals, which were loftier than anyone could have reason to believe.

And who knows? If Mo Lewis hadn't speared Drew Bledsoe where he did, when he did, maybe Brady wouldn't have had his chance. Pro sports—and the NFL in particular—are littered with stories of what-might-have-beens. But when Brady got his opportunity, he clung to it as though his life depended on it.

In his first 17 seasons as the Patriots' starter, he led them to the Super Bowl at nearly an every-other-year pace, winning eight conference championships. That's more conference titles than any team outside the Pittsburgh Steelers, who also have won eight in the Super Bowl era.

In the first two Super Bowls Brady didn't win, he led the Patriots to scores in the closing minutes that put his team ahead, only to have the New England defense fail to preserve the lead. In the third, he passed for a playoff-record 505 yards and was driving down the field in search of a potential game-tying touchdown when time ran out.

Brady is at his best in the biggest games. He has played in and won more postseason games than any quarterback in league history, and his four Super Bowl MVP Awards are also unmatched. He once went 10 straight postseason games, spread out over four seasons, without a loss. In total, no quarterback in NFL history has thrown more touchdown passes, attempted and completed more passes, and amassed more yardage in the playoffs.

Even at age 40, when Brady won his third MVP award and led the Pats to Super Bowl LII, he still possessed a deft touch and the ability to throw the long ball. He still served as an adjunct coach on the field, seeing things others didn't, or at the very least before they did. On the sideline, he still exhorted, cajoled, and motivated his teammates, and they still trusted in him.

The debate about whether Brady is the NFL's greatest quarterback of all time seems almost quaint now, after his miraculous rebound from a 28–3 second-half deficit in Super Bowl LI. Next up: whether Brady can, as he vows, to continue to play at an elite level until age 45.

Go ahead and snicker. It will only motivate him further.

How great was Tom Brady?

At the age of 39, when most quarterbacks are either retired or serving as backups, Brady established the best touchdown-to-interception ratio for a quarterback in NFL history, connecting for 28 touchdowns against only two picks.

Bobby *ORR*

DEFENSEMAN - BOSTON BRUINS (1966—1976)

Robert Gordon Orr was 14 years old when he signed with the Bruins. Repeat: 14. He wasn't old enough to drive, much less drink, but the Bruins rightly determined that even at that tender age, he was one of the most amazing talents they had seen.

They weren't wrong.

Signed as a kid, Orr made his NHL debut four years later and grew into a man who would change the history not only of the Bruins, but also the sport itself.

Until Orr came along, defensemen were implicitly forbidden from joining the offensive attack. Their sole responsibility had been to help the goaltender keep the puck out of his own net.

Evidently Orr saw that as insufficiently ambitious. If he already had possession of the puck, why not do something productive with it? Why chip the puck out of the zone or zip a pass to a forward on the move, when he himself could get it from point A to point B faster than anyone?

And, oh, how he could skate. There were others in the game, like Jean Beliveau, who could glide with an almost regal elegance. Or like Maurice Richard or Bobby Hull, who could come barreling down the wing in short bursts, brandishing powerful shots to go with their speed.

But Orr turned hockey into a 200-foot game. He could strip the puck from an opponent, retreat behind his net, and like a jet plane revving up, begin his approach. He would elude forecheckers, offer a head feint, and zip past flat-footed defenders.

On occasion, he would accelerate into a higher gear—fifth? sixth?—whose very existence was unknown, dangling the puck close to his stick, with its trademark single strand of black tape, as if he were taunting his opponents. The length of the ice would be littered by beaten opponents, all victims of a hockey hit-and-run.

Orr put up numbers that were, frankly, cartoonish. In 1968–69, his third season, he broke the record for most points in a season by a defenseman with 64. The following season, he nearly doubled that total with 120. His 87 assists alone that season would have easily established a record for most points by a defenseman, but that didn't even include the 33 goals he tallied.

In 1969–70, at the ripe age of 21, Orr led the Bruins to their first Stanley Cup title since World War II, and two years later he did it again.

By then, knee injuries had taken their toll. Each surgical procedure reduced him somewhat, as though the hockey gods had found a cruel manner in which to level the ice against his natural talent. By the time he was 30 Orr's career was effectively over.

Maybe that was sadly fitting. Orr, as was his style on the ice, was like a streaking comet who came and went before we fully understood what we had witnessed.

How great was Bobby Orr?

In 1970–71, Orr compiled a plus-124 rating, meaning he was on the ice for 124 more even-strength goals scored by his team than allowed. In all of hockey history, only two other players have ever had a plus-minus greater than 100 in a season.

Bill *RUSSELL*

CENTER - BOSTON CELTICS (1956–1969)

As much as we love sports, as much as we anticipate each game, as much as we savor great individual performances, it's shockingly easy to lose sight of the ultimate goal, the reason the games get played in the first place.

We revel in the highlights, marvel at the improbable play, and celebrate the performance. *Did you see that?*

We debate who is best, who is toughest, who is strongest, who is fastest. We have our favorite players, for whom we root.

Through the hero worship, the obsession with our superstars, we sometimes lose the plot and forget the whole object of the competition in the first place:

To win.

Bill Russell never forgot.

Forget? It became his raison d'etre. And Russell won more—more consistently, longer, and almost without interruption—than any other major sport athlete in modern history.

Consider: he won two consecutive NCAA championships with the University of San Francisco before joining the US Olympic team, which won the gold medal at the 1956 Games. He then joined the Celtics and, in a run that is unparalleled in North American professional sports, proceeded to win 11 titles over the next 13 seasons. In the two years he didn't win, the Celtics lost in the NBA Finals in one and in the conference finals in the other.

In sum: over the course of 15 college and pro seasons, Russell won 13 championships and competed strongly for two others. And as the cherry on top, he added an Olympic gold medal.

For Russell, winning wasn't merely habit forming; it was his oxygen, his drug of choice. He wasn't concerned with personal glory or gaudy statistics. He never came close to leading the league in scoring, and frankly, he couldn't have cared less.

Russell was the embodiment of a team player. But he wasn't just a benchwarmer, some towel-waiving extra contributing from the sidelines because he wasn't good enough to be on the court. No, Russell was a fierce defender, a determined rebounder, and above all else, a relentless competitor.

Let others worry about individual glory. Russell had loftier goals.

"The most important measure of how good a game I played," he once said, "was how much better I made my teammates play."

The Celtics hadn't won an NBA championship until Russell arrived. They won a title in his first season, and bookended that, 12 seasons later, when they won in his final year. After Russell retired, the Celtics didn't win again for another five seasons.

Sense a pattern here?

Beyond his obsession with winning, Russell helped pioneer the Celtics' fast-break style by smothering opponents on defense, corralling rebounds, and firing outlet passes downcourt to streaking teammates.

He played with intensity, with commitment, and with immense pride. He subjugated his own ego and accomplishments for a common goal, principally because he never forgot the object of competing in the first place.

"The only important statistic is the final score," he said.

How great was Bill Russell?

From 1951 through 1957, Russell won two state high school championships, two NCAA championships, one Olympic gold medal, and one NBA championship. Given that college freshmen were ineligible in the 1950s, Russell won six championships in seven years at every level at which he competed.

Ted WILLIAMS

LEFT FIELDER - BOSTON RED SOX (1939–1942, 1946–1960)

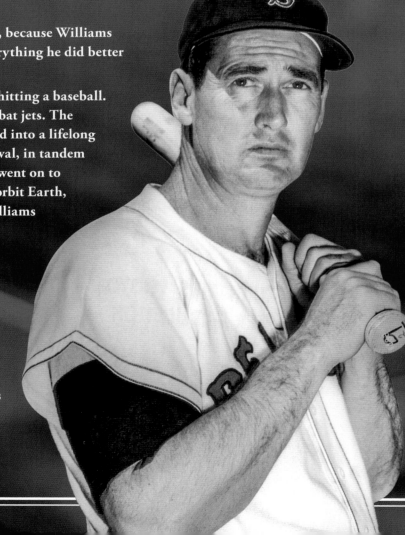

It has been called the hardest thing to do in sports: The practice of hitting a round ball with a round bat. Harder than lofting a spiral 30 yards in the air with precision. Harder than drilling a jumper with a defender in your face. Harder than stopping a 100 mph slap shot arriving through traffic.

It just so happens that Ted Williams was better at it than anyone else who had ever tried.

Perhaps that shouldn't be surprising, because Williams made it a point, a goal, a need, to do everything he did better than anyone else.

That commitment wasn't limited to hitting a baseball. It also applied to fishing and flying combat jets. The former began as an avocation and evolved into a lifelong pursuit. The latter was done out of survival, in tandem with John Glenn, in Korea. Glenn, who went on to become the first American astronaut to orbit Earth, was unashamed to acknowledge that Williams was the superior pilot.

But Williams saved his best for the batter's box.

The other aspects of the game, frankly, could disinterest him at times. During lulls of play in left field, he could be seen practicing his swing. Defense was something he had to do in between at-bats. Base running? That was a means to an end.

But hitting was Williams's real passion. He studied it, researched it, and came as close as anyone to perfecting it. It was no accident that his most famous treatise was *The Science of Hitting* because for Williams, success at the plate was not happenstance.

Decades before it became popular, Williams invented the concept of "hot zones"—the areas of the strike zone where he was most successful. He preached patience and discipline long before anyone understood the value of on-base percentage. And long before talk of "launch angles" became common, he emphasized the need to hit the ball in the air.

In some respects he was the anti–Bill Russell. While the Celtics center won with a metronomic regularity, Williams never won a single championship in his major league career, which spanned parts of four decades.

Williams can't be held solely responsible for that hole in his résumé. Too often, the Red Sox lacked the necessary pitching to compete for a World Series, and in the latter half of his career in Boston, ownership and management were too stubborn, too reluctant, too *something* to welcome black players onto their roster.

But make no mistake: when Williams was in the batter's box, he had no equal.

He remains baseball's last .400 hitter, a distinction that has stood for more than three-quarters of a century. In 19 seasons he never hit below .300. That streak ended in 1959, his second-to-last season, before he improbably rebounded to hit .316 in 1960 at age 41.

His 521 homers, good enough for third place all-time when he retired, would have been far greater had he not missed parts of five seasons due to military service. There's little doubt that he would have easily topped the 600-homer milestone and could well have challenged Babe Ruth's 714.

But no number or statistic could fully capture or define his greatness at the plate.

Wrote Williams: "A man has to have goals—for a day, for a lifetime—and that was mine, to have people say, 'There goes Ted Williams, the greatest hitter who ever lived.'"

Damned if he didn't achieve that goal.

How great was Ted Williams?

Over the course of his career, Williams recorded an on-base percentage of .482, meaning that, in nearly 8,000 plate appearances, he achieved the goal of reaching base safely—which, after all, is the goal of every hitter—almost half the time.

INDEX

ABOUT THE AUTHOR

Sean McAdam is a nationally known, award-winning sportswriter who has covered the Boston sports scene for nearly four decades. He's written for the *Providence Journal*, the *Boston Herald, Comcast SportsNet New England, Boston Sports Journal, ESPN.com*, and *FoxSports.com* and regularly appears on 98.5 WBZ-FM. He's covered the Boston Red Sox for the last 30 years. He lives in Massachusetts with his wife, Suzanne, and their children.

ACKNOWLEDGMENTS

I've been fortunate enough to have had terrific editors (and bosses) throughout my career, each of whom instilled important lessons along the way. I want to thank, in particular, Dave Reid, Dave Bloss, Arthur Martone, Hank Hryniewicz, and Greg Bedard for their invaluable support and guidance over the years.

For this project in particular, I owe everything to the editor, Chrös McDougall, who displayed unfailing patience and invaluable assistance to a first-time author. A special thank-you, too, goes to Josh Fowler, who was kind enough to recommend me for this assignment, and without whom I would never have been involved in this rewarding project.